T0006040

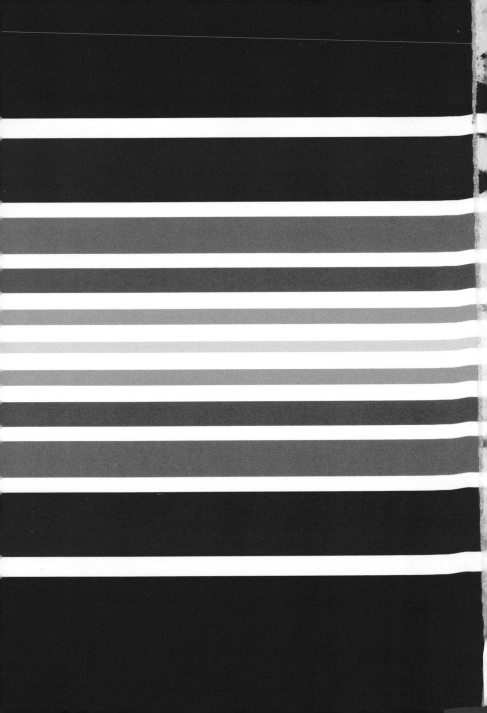

YOU CAN COUNT ON GOD

100 Devotions for Kids

MAX LUCADO

ADAPTED FOR CHILDREN BY TAMA FORTNER

THOMAS NELSON
Since 1798

You Can Count on God

© 2022 Max Lucado

Tommy Nelson, PO Box 141000, Nashville, TN 37214

All rights reserved. No portion of this book may be reproduced, stored in a retrieval system, or transmitted in any form or by any means—electronic, mechanical, photocopy, recording, scanning, or other—except for brief quotations in critical reviews or articles, without the prior written permission of the publisher.

Published in Nashville, Tennessee, by Tommy Nelson. Tommy Nelson is an imprint of Thomas Nelson. Thomas Nelson is a registered trademark of HarperCollins Christian Publishing, Inc.

Adapted for children by Tama Fortner.

The adaptor is represented by Cyle Young of C.Y.L.E. (Cyle Young Literary Elite, LLC), a literary agency.

Tommy Nelson titles may be purchased in bulk for educational, business, fund-raising, or sales promotional use. For information, please email SpecialMarkets@ThomasNelson.com.

Unless otherwise noted, Scripture quotations are taken from the International Children's Bible®. Copyright © 1986, 1988, 1999, 2015, by Thomas Nelson. Used by permission. All rights reserved.

Scripture quotations marked ESV are taken from the ESV® Bible (The Holy Bible, English Standard Version®), © 2001 by Crossway, a publishing ministry of Good News Publishers. Used by permission. All rights reserved.

Scripture quotations marked NCV are taken from the New Century Version®. Copyright © 2005 by Thomas Nelson. Used by permission. All rights reserved.

Scripture quotations marked NIV are taken from the Holy Bible, New International Version®, NIV®. Copyright © 1973, 1978, 1984, 2011 by Biblica, Inc.® Used by permission of Zondervan. All rights reserved worldwide. www.Zondervan. com. The "NIV" and "New International Version" are trademarks registered in the United States Patent and Trademark Office by Biblica, Inc.®

Scripture quotations marked NLT are taken from the Holy Bible, New Living Translation. © 1996, 2004, 2015 by Tyndale House Foundation. Used by permission of Tyndale House Ministries, Carol Stream, Illinois 60188. All rights reserved.

ISBN 978-1-4002-3330-4 (audiobook)
ISBN 978-1-4002-3331-1 (eBook)
ISBN 978-1-4002-3332-8 (HC)

Library of Congress Cataloging-in-Publication Data

Names: Lucado, Max, author. | Fortner, Tama, 1969- author.
Title: You can count on God : 100 devotions / Max Lucado ; adapted by Tama Fortner.
Description: Nashville, TN : Thomas Nelson, [2022] | Includes bibliographical references. | Audience: Ages 6-10 | Summary: "Help kids worry less, bravely try new things, and draw closer to God as they learn to trust His faithfulness with 100 devotions for children from New York Times bestselling author Max Lucado"-- Provided by publisher.
Identifiers: LCCN 2021033382 (print) | LCCN 2021033383 (ebook) | ISBN 9781400233328 (hc) | ISBN 9781400233311 (ebook) | ISBN 9781400233304 audiobook)
Subjects: LCSH: Christian children--Prayers and devotions--Juvenile literature. | Christian children--Religious life--Juvenile literature. | Trust in God--Christianity--Juvenile literature.
Classification: LCC BV4870 .L83 2022 (print) | LCC BV4870 (ebook) | DDC 242/.62--dc23
LC record available at https://lccn.loc.gov/2021033382
LC ebook record available at https://lccn.loc.gov/2021033383

Printed in Italy

24 25 26 RTL 6 5 4 3

Mfr: Rotolito S.p.A. / Milan / January 2024 /PO#12249574

A GIFT FOR:

_____

FROM:

_____

DATE:

_____

A LETTER FROM MAX

Hi, friend,

I have a question for you: Who do you count on?

When you get scared, who do you count on to help overcome your fear? When someone hurts your feelings, is there someone you turn to?

Or, when something awesome happens in your life and you want to jump up and down and let out a big whoop, who do you want to celebrate with?

You might have said parents, brothers, sisters, grandparents, friends, teachers. And those would be great answers. I hope you have people like that in your life to share both tough days and happy times.

But I really hope number one on your list is your heavenly Father. Why? Because no matter what happens in life, God wants to know about it. He wants to share your fears, your pain, and your joys. Your heavenly Father loves celebrating you. He's your best friend when you're sad, and the one you can turn to with your worries.

So, no matter what's going on in your world: good, bad, happy, sad, always remember: you can count on God.

I sure do.

Your friend,
Max

1

TUCKED UNDER GOD'S WINGS

[God] will protect you like a bird
spreading its wings over its young.

PSALM 91:4

Have you ever seen a mama bird covering her babies with her wings? That mama bird was protecting her chicks. No raindrops were going to splash them. No wind was going to make them cold. And most important, no enemy was going to snatch them away. Not while mama bird was around.

When King David was a boy, he was a shepherd. He took care of his father's sheep. David spent lots of days in the fields. And he probably saw plenty of baby birds tucked up under their mamas' wings. Maybe that's why David thought of a mama bird when he wrote about how God protects us.

David knew all about protection. Since he was a shepherd, a big part of his job was to keep the sheep safe. Hungry lions prowled around, hoping to steal a meal. And there were wild bears just waiting for a snack. Those lions and bears were much bigger and stronger than David was. It was David's job to protect the sheep, but who protected David?

God did!

When danger came around, God sheltered David just like a mama bird covering her little ones with her wings. God's wings aren't made of feathers, though. They are made of his strength, courage, and love. David knew it was God who kept him safe. He said, "The Lord saved me from a lion and a bear" (1 Samuel 17:37).

Chances are you won't face a bear in your backyard or a lion in the lunchroom. But you just might have a bear of a big test that's worrying you. Or maybe your scary lion is searching for someone to sit with in a new school. Whatever you're facing, remember how God protected David. You can trust him to cover you with his strength, courage, and love too.

IT'S YOUR TURN!

Roll a pinecone in peanut butter, then birdseed. Hang it outside. As you watch the birds enjoy the snack, remember how God covers you with his wings.

2

UP, DOWN, AND
ALL AROUND

*The heavens tell the glory of God. And the skies
announce what his hands have made. Day after day
they tell the story. Night after night they tell it again.*

PSALM 19:1–2

I f you want to know that God is real, all you have to do is look up,
look down, and look all around. Take a close look at a blade of grass
or a leaf on a tree. How did it know what color it should be? Look at
all the tiny details of a snowflake. Who carved those? Feel the wind on
your face. How does it know which way to blow? Follow the butterfly
as it floats along. Who painted its wings with all those colors? Who
put the stars in the sky? Who told the moon to shine? How did oceans
and clown fish and anemones come to be?

Look up, look down, and look all around. The evidence is

everywhere! You can ask a million questions—and then a million more—about who and how. And the answer to every one would be the same: God.

Some people say the universe, the earth, and everything in it—even you and I—just happened. It was an accident and a mystery. But all you have to do is look around and see that just isn't true.

God wants his people to know him. So he planted the proof that he is real in every flower and tree. He carved it into every snowflake. And he painted it on every butterfly's wing. His faithfulness—his promise to always be there—shines through the sun that rises every morning and the moon that lights up the night. And his love makes sure that even the tiniest bird has food and a cozy nest.

So if you ever wonder if God is real, if he really cares, just look—up, down, and all around. The evidence is everywhere! God is real. God is the Creator. And God loves his creation, especially you and me.

IT'S YOUR TURN!

Grab a magnifying glass and head outside. Check out a leaf, a flower petal, or a butterfly's wing. Look at your own fingers. Do you see God's wonderful designs?

3

PARTNERS AFTER THE CRIME

If we confess our sins, he will forgive our sins.

1 JOHN 1:9

Guilt. It first popped up in the garden of Eden with Adam and Eve. The devil slipped in like a serpent and tricked those two into snacking on the one fruit God had said not to eat. The devil said it would make them like God. He lied. (The devil does that a *lot*.)

When Adam and Eve heard God walking in the garden, they knew they had done wrong, and they felt guilty. It was a horrible new feeling for them. Then they began to worry. What would God say when he found out what they had done? So Adam and Eve ran away to hide.

Of course, God found them. The truth came out. And yes, they got into trouble. But even then, God took care of them. He gave them clothes to wear and a way to get food to eat. And he already had a plan to wash away their sin.

When you do the things you know are wrong, the guilt comes first. You knew you shouldn't have told that lie, picked that fight, or pretended to be sick to skip school. But you did, and now you feel terrible. Those guilty feelings are so huge you're sure everyone can see them. And with all that guilt comes worry. *Will I get caught? Will anyone find out?*

Guilt and worry. They're partners in crime. Or maybe I should say they're partners *after* the crime. Because it's after you choose to do wrong that these feelings gang up on you.

There's a surefire way to send these two partners packing. *Confess.* Tell what you did. I know it sounds crazy, but trust me. When the thing you're most afraid of happens—when the truth comes out—guilt and worry lose their power over you. So tell God all about it and ask him to forgive you. (He will!) Tell the person you've wronged that you're sorry. Then do what you can to make it right.

PRAY

God, I'm sorry for the wrong things I've done.
Thank you for forgiving me. Amen.

4

THE WAY GOD WANTS IT TO BE

*God made a promise to us. And we are waiting
for what he promised—a new heaven and
a new earth where goodness lives.*

2 PETER 3:13

This world is a mess. But it's not supposed to be.

In the beginning, when God made the heavens and the earth and everything in them—including you and me—it was all good (Genesis 1). But then along came a slippery snake named Satan, whose sneaky ways led Adam and Eve to make a meal out of the one fruit they were not supposed to eat. That's when sin came into the world and messed everything up.

But every once in a while, you can see a little bit of how it's supposed to be. God's goodness *is* still here in this world. Look for it in a kitten's purr and a puppy's wagging tail. See it in a smile and feel it in the hug of someone you love.

Yes, this world is a mess. But God sent Jesus to begin making things new. He's already defeated sin and death. And when Jesus comes back again, everything will be the way God made it to be. Mice will be pals with cats, and lambs will curl up with wolves to take a nap. Lions won't snarl. Bears won't growl. And sharks won't bite. There won't be any more earthquakes, tornadoes, or thunderstorms.

No more hurting. No more sadness. No more fussing or fighting or selfishness. Just love and light and joy and—best of all—God. Until that day comes, let the love and goodness of God shine out of you. Give the world a glimpse of how God wants it to be.

This world is definitely a mess. But one day it won't be. And I, for one, can't wait to see it!

REMEMBER

God promises us in Revelations 21:5 that
he is making all things new!

5

LOOK AT HIM!

Do everything for the glory of God.

1 CORINTHIANS 10:31

Look at my report card!" you call to your mom so she can see your high marks.

"Watch this!" you tell your friends as you do a trick on your skateboard. And they all say, "Watch this!" right back to you.

We all want to be seen. Even grown-ups. So here's some wonderful news: God always sees you.

Just ask Hagar. She was the servant of Abraham and Sarah. When Hagar was going to have a baby, Sarah became very jealous because she couldn't have any babies of her own. So Sarah treated Hagar terribly. It became so bad that Hagar ran away into the desert. But God saw her, even there. He sent his angel to help her and to give her a promise: her baby would one day be the father of so many descendants they cannot be counted.

Hagar gave the Lord a new name that day. She called Him *El Roi*. It means "the God who sees me."

God *does* see you. No matter where you are. And he wants you to help others see him. When others look at you, he doesn't just want them to see how high you can swing, how fast you ride your bike, or how great you are on the trampoline. God wants you to show them a little bit of him—in the way you treat others, in the kind words you say, in the way you help and give and forgive.

Sure, it's okay to sometimes say, "Look at me!" But be sure that when others see you, they also see a little bit of him.

PRAY

God, help me do and say things that help other
people see how good you are. Amen.

6

TRICKS, TRAPS, AND LIES

Give yourselves to God. Stand against the devil,
and the devil will run away from you.

JAMES 4:7

The devil is a really sneaky fellow. And he's always up to no good. He's got more tricks than a magician. His traps are more dangerous than any hunter's. And when it comes to lying, he's really good.

The devil uses all those tricks and traps and lies to get you to mess up. He's hoping you'll choose to do what is wrong instead of what is right. In other words, he really wants you to sin. Why? Because sin pulls you away from God. And that's what the devil wants most of all.

But God tells you exactly how to get rid of that devil guy—with prayer, praise, and God's holy Word.

When you pray, you ask God to fight for you. (And there's no doubt about who will win that fight—God! He wins every single time!) As soon as you start talking to God, the devil knows that God is on his way to help. That's when he gets worried and starts slinking away.

When you praise God, you do something that the devil can't stand to do. You tell God how wonderful and amazing he is. You tell him that you know he has all the power and that he can do anything. And you thank him for all the ways he loves and blesses you. Whether you sing it, shout it, or just think it in your thoughts, praise makes the devil plug up his ears.

When you read and learn the truths of God's Word, you cut right through the devil's lies. That's why God's Word is called the sword of the Spirit (Ephesians 6:17). It can help you see what is true and right, and it can teach you what God wants you to do.

So if that devil starts sneaking around, say a prayer, shout out a praise, or simply read the truths of God's Word. And the devil won't stick around.

REMEMBER

Prayer and praise make the devil run away!

7

GOD'S GOT A PLAN

*[God] chose us in advance, and he makes
everything work out according to his plan.*

EPHESIANS 1:11 NLT

Joseph had it all. He was his father's favorite son. He had this amazing coat of many colors. And he had these dreams about how his entire family would bow down to him one day. But Joseph had one other thing too—a bunch of jealous brothers. They got tired of Joseph's fancy coat and big dreams. So they sold him as a slave to some traders headed toward Egypt.

In Egypt, Joseph worked hard, and his master began to trust him. Things were starting to look good for him. At least until his boss's wife said Joseph did something he didn't do. The next thing Joseph knew, he was sitting in a jail cell.

Why did God let all those bad things happen? Why did he let Joseph be sold as a slave and then get thrown into prison? Because that wasn't the end of Joseph's story. God worked through all those terrible things to do something wonderful.

In prison, Joseph met the butler of the king of Egypt. And with God's help, Joseph told the butler the meaning of a dream he'd had. So later, when the king needed help understanding a dream, the butler remembered Joseph. Before you could say "pumpernickel," Joseph went from prison to the palace, where he was put in charge of all Egypt, second in command after the king. He saved the people of Egypt and even his own family—including those kidnapping brothers of his—from starving in a famine.

Years later, Joseph told his brothers, "You meant to hurt me. But God turned your evil into good. It was to save the lives of many people" (Genesis 50:20).

So the next time you've got troubles and you don't see how things could ever be good again, don't give up. Trust God. He's got a plan. And he's always working for your good.

IT'S YOUR TURN!

When everything was going wrong for Joseph, he still chose to do right. When you're having a bad day, what right things can you do? Here's a hint: check out Micah 6:8.

8

ALL THE TIME, NO MATTER WHAT

"I give you a new command: Love each other. You must love each other as I have loved you."

JOHN 13:34

Be nice. Stop arguing. Just get along. Chances are if you have a brother or sister, or even a buddy you hang out with a lot, you've heard those words from the adults in your life. More than once. And if you're anything like my brother and me when we were kids, you've probably heard them a lot.

God doesn't want us just to get along with others, though. He wants us to love them. And not just any old kind of love. He wants us to love others the way he loves us. Which is all the time, no matter what.

How is that even possible? Some people aren't all that nice. They're kind of grouchy or selfish, or just plain mean. Maybe you wonder if God has ever met your brother, your sister, your neighbor down the street. How can he expect you to love someone like that?

The answer is at the end of John 13:34: "as I have loved you." How does God love you? It's no ordinary kind of love. It doesn't depend on what you do, what you say, or what you wear. God loves you with an *agape* kind of love. That means he loves you no matter what. Period. End of story.

How much does God love you? More than a bear loves honey, more than a fish loves water, more than I love homemade ice cream on the Fourth of July. His love for you stretches farther than the edge of outer space. It's bigger than the mountains and wider than all the seas. God loves you like he loves Jesus, his own Son (John 17:23). And he's made you part of his family (1 John 3:1).

God's got so much love for you that there's more than enough to share. Don't just get along. Love the people around you.

REMEMBER

God's *agape* kind of love means he
loves you—no matter what!

9

"I AM" IS WITH YOU

"Call to me in times of trouble. I will save you."

PSALM 50:15

There's a lot to read about Moses in the Bible. He first appears as a tiny Israelite baby. His mother sent him off in a basket, sailing down the Nile River, to save his life. He was rescued by a princess of Egypt. So even though all the other Hebrews in the land were slaves, Moses grew up as a prince in a palace. But Moses was still a Hebrew in his heart. When he tried to defend a Hebrew slave, he killed an Egyptian. Afraid that the Egyptian king would try to kill him, he ran away into the wilderness.

That's where Moses became a shepherd. And that's where Moses met God. It wasn't the usual sort of meeting. There was no "Hello. Nice to meet you" or "I haven't seen you around here before." This meeting started with a bush, crackling with flames of fire. *But it did not burn up!*

Moses spotted this bush and knew he had to get a closer look. The bush spoke—or rather, God spoke from the bush: "Moses, Moses!" (Exodus 3:4). I'm guessing that's when Moses realized this was not going to be just another day with the sheep.

God had a mission for Moses: go back to Egypt, lead his people out of that land, and lead them to a better place. But Moses wasn't sure about that plan. Why would the Israelites trust him?

That's when God said, "When you go to the people of Israel, tell them, 'I AM sent me to you'" (v. 14).

I AM had a special meaning in the Hebrew language, the language of the Israelites. It means that God always lives and is always with his people. *Always.* That means back there in the desert with Moses, and it means right here today. Whenever you're worried or upset or scared or just having the worst day, call to him. Then remember that I AM is with you and he will lead you to a better place.

PRAY

God, you are the great I AM. You have always been and will always be. And best of all, you are always with me. Amen.

10

BIG AND BOLD
AND AMAZING

"Don't be afraid. I am with you."

ISAIAH 43:5

Long ago, God made a promise to his people. When you choose to follow him, you become one of his people—and that promise becomes yours too.

Want to know what that promise is? God will take care of you (Isaiah 43:1–5). And because he is God, he is able to do it. No matter what kind of trouble comes your way. Why does God take care of you? That's the best part! It's because *you are precious to him* (v. 4).

Sometimes God keeps his promise in little ways, like sending a friend to cheer you up on a tough day. Other times, God works in ways you can't see. Like going ahead of you and getting rid of a problem before you even know it's there. But sometimes he works in ways that are big and bold and amazing! Like what he did for the Israelites at the Red Sea.

God had just helped the Israelites escape from slavery in Egypt. He told Moses to lead them down to the Red Sea. Then, the Egyptian king decided he wanted his slaves back. He sent his army after them. The Israelites were trapped between the army and the sea.

What would you do if you were one of those Israelites? Panic? Try to swim across? Hide behind a tree? They didn't have to do any of those things. God stepped in and took care of them by parting the sea. He sent winds to blow back the waters until there was a path of dry ground right through the middle of the sea. Amazing!

If you find yourself stuck and big trouble is headed your way, don't be afraid. Trust God. Tell him your fears. Then watch to see how he takes care of you. It might be in a little way or a way you can't see. Or it just might be big and bold and amazing!

PRAY

God, thank you for all the ways you take care of
me—little, invisible, and big, bold, and amazing!

11

IF GOD SAYS IT . . .

We can trust God to do what he promised.

HEBREWS 10:23

You may have heard stories about how Joshua defeated the city of Jericho. But that's not *exactly* how things happened. It was more like God *gave* Joshua the city of Jericho. Here's what really happened.

After their escape from slavery in Egypt, the Israelites wandered in the wilderness for forty years. They didn't do this because they liked the wilderness. It was their punishment for not going into the promised land the first time God told them to. Now, forty years later, the Israelites were back at the edge of the promised land. And this time they were ready to do what God said.

The first city they faced was the mighty city of Jericho. All around that great city stood a huge, tall, stone wall. Joshua, the Israelites' leader, knew it would be a hard battle just to get over that wall.

But God had a plan. Honestly, it was a pretty strange plan.

But Joshua had seen God do some amazing things, and he trusted God. Joshua knew God would do what he said he would do. So the Israelites followed God's plan. Instead of rushing into battle, they simply marched around the city of Jericho every day for six days. On the seventh day, they marched around the city seven times. Then the priests blew their trumpets, the people gave a great shout, and the mighty walls of Jericho came crashing down! God said he would give the city to his people, and that's exactly what he did.

God always—*always*—keeps his promises. Even when they seem a little bit crazy. If God says he will do it, he will. Because it is impossible for God to lie (Hebrews 6:18). A rock cannot swim. A hippo cannot fly. A butterfly cannot eat a bowl of spaghetti. You cannot sleep on a cloud, and God cannot lie.

If God says he will do it, he will. You can always count on him.

IT'S YOUR TURN!

There's something else God told Joshua he would do. And it's a promise he gives to you too. Find out what it is in Joshua 1:9.

12

THE STORY OF
YOU AND JESUS

*This is what the Lord says. . . . "Don't be
afraid, because I have saved you. I have called
you by name, and you are mine."*

ISAIAH 43:1

Bethlehem was hit by a terrible famine. Crops were not growing, and food was getting hard to find. So Naomi, her husband,
and her two sons moved to the land of Moab. Her two sons married
women from that land. Then Naomi's husband died, and her two sons
died not long after that. Naomi was left alone with her two daughters-
in-law, Ruth and Orpah. With her heart broken and her family gone,
Naomi decided to go back to Bethlehem. Orpah went back to her own
family, but Ruth went with Naomi.

Because Naomi and Ruth were widows and because they were

poor, life was not easy. Ruth went out into the fields. There she gathered up the bits of grain that the workers dropped. She and Naomi baked the grain into bread for their food. No one paid much attention to Naomi and Ruth. No one really tried to help them.

Except Boaz. Boaz was not poor. In fact, he was quite rich. He owned the fields where Ruth gathered her grain. Boaz saw Ruth. He asked others about her and learned her story. Boaz spoke to her with kindness, helped her, and protected her. Then Boaz married Ruth, saving her and Naomi from a life of struggle.

Did you know that the story of Ruth and Boaz is a lot like the story of you and Jesus? Boaz *saw* Ruth. Jesus *sees* you—he even knows every hair on your head! Boaz was rich. Jesus owns every inch of the universe. Boaz told the workers to leave Ruth alone. Jesus tells Satan to leave you alone. Boaz saved Ruth and Naomi from struggle. Jesus saves you from sin. Boaz took Ruth into his home. Jesus wants to take you into his.

And all you need to do is see and love and follow him.

PRAY

Thank you, Lord, for seeing me, for protecting
me, and for sending Jesus to save me. Amen.

13

A GREAT IDEA

*I praise you because you made me in an
amazing and wonderful way. What you have
done is wonderful. I know this very well.*

PSALM 139:14

You are a *great* idea! I don't mean you *have* great ideas—though I'm sure you do! I mean that you yourself are a great idea. How do I know that? Because you are God's idea—and he only has great ideas.

When God sat down to create the very first man and woman, he said, "Let us make human beings in our image and likeness" (Genesis 1:26). God didn't say, "Let us make oceans in our image" or "flowers in our likeness" or "giraffes in our likeness." Nothing else in all of God's creation is made in his likeness. Not plants, or weeds, or trees. Not elephants, anteaters, or even the cutest little puppy. Not stars, or mountains, or seas. Only people—including you and me.

What does it mean to be made in God's likeness? It means you are made to look like him. Maybe not on the outside. But on the inside, in your heart and mind and soul. Does that mean you're perfect? Nope, nobody is. Except Jesus, of course. But it does mean that you take after him. You get your kindness and your courage from him. And when you love and help and forgive others, that's when you look the most like him.

In this world, people will sometimes see your mistakes as a reason to laugh at you. Some people might call you names. Others might decide not to be your friend because of where you live or the way you look. Don't listen to them. Instead, remember this: You are made in the image of God. You're a diamond, a precious jewel. You are so important to God, so loved by him, that he sent his only Son to save you.

You can't see them, but God's fingerprints are all over you. So be sure to thank God today for his great idea of making you!

REMEMBER

You are God's great idea!

14

BE C.A.L.M.

*God's peace will keep your hearts and minds
in Christ Jesus. The peace that God gives is
so great that we cannot understand it.*

PHILIPPIANS 4:7

There's a lot of worry going around in this world. Even for kids! No matter how old you are, you worry about things like fitting in. You worry about whether your friends still want to be your friends. You worry about homework and chores and how your family is doing. And sometimes things from the grown-up world can creep in and worry you.

Carrying around all that worry can be like carrying around a backpack loaded with rocks. Do you want to put down that backpack? Toss out some rocks? Let me tell you how. Be C.A.L.M.

I know, I know. Just telling someone to be calm isn't very helpful. Especially when they're stressed-out with worry. But "be calm" isn't the answer. It's what "C.A.L.M." stands for that is the answer. Check this out:

> *C is for celebrate.* When you start counting up all the reasons God gives you to celebrate, you forget to be worried. The Bible says it this way: "Be full of joy in the Lord always" (Philippians 4:4).
>
> *A is for ask.* Ask God for his help. In other words, "Pray and ask God for everything you need" (v. 6). God will take care of you.
>
> *L is for leave.* Leave your worries with him. "Do not worry about anything" (v. 6) because God has everything under control.
>
> *M is for meditate.* And *meditate* is just a fancy way of saying think about. God wants you to "think about the things that are good and worthy of praise" (v. 8). Because when your mind is all filled up with thoughts of good things, there's no room for worry.

When you celebrate, ask, leave, and meditate—when you are C.A.L.M.—God takes away those worrying thoughts. And he fills you up with his peace instead.

IT'S YOUR TURN!

When worry starts dragging you down, write it down. Make a list of everything that's worrying you. Then, make another list. This time write down all the wonderful gifts from God that are all around you. Which one is bigger?

15

SIDE BY SIDE

Encourage each other and build each other up.

1 THESSALONIANS 5:11 NLT

Naomi had lost so much: her homeland, her husband, and both her sons. She wasn't just sad; she was heartbroken. Her money was gone and—even worse—her hope was gone. Naomi just wanted to go back to her home in Bethlehem.

Ruth and Orpah had been married to Naomi's sons. When Naomi's sons died, Naomi told the women to go back to their own families because she had nothing left to offer them. She had decided that she would travel all the way to Bethlehem alone. Orpah left, but Ruth stayed.

Ruth didn't have money or power. She couldn't fix Naomi's problems for her. But she could stay with her, stand by her, and walk beside her all the way back to Bethlehem. Ruth could make sure that

Naomi didn't have to face the world all on her own. And that is no small thing. In fact, it's really huge.

Sometimes encouraging others means being a cheerleader and lending a helping hand. And sometimes it means sharing a lot of good and helpful words to wash away the bad and hurtful words that a person has heard.

But often, encouraging someone means not saying anything at all. It's simply walking beside someone—down the sidewalk, across the lunchroom, or when they're going somewhere they don't really want to go. Sometimes it's sharing a snack or meal together—so that person doesn't have to eat alone. It can be sitting with someone and listening to their story. And sometimes encouraging someone means simply being with them, not saying a word, and letting them know you'll always be right there by their side.

REMEMBER

Walk beside, sit with, listen to—you can
encourage others without saying a word.

16

GOOD THINGS
FROM GOD

*You have been saved by grace because you believe. You
did not save yourselves. It was a gift from God.*

EPHESIANS 2:8

What's the biggest thing you can think of? An elephant? The
ocean? The whole world? How about the entire universe?
Double it, and God's love would still be bigger. Triple it, and you still
wouldn't even be close. Multiply it by a hundred—a thousand—a
million!—and God's love would still be so, so, so much bigger.

And it's because of God's great, big, enormous love for us that he
offers us grace.

What is grace? you ask.

Grace is getting good things from God. We don't deserve them.
There's no way we could earn these things for ourselves. And we could

never, ever, ever pay God back for them. What are these good things? They're forgiveness for our sins, the Holy Spirit coming to live inside us to help us, and getting to live with God in heaven one day.

Why do we need God's grace? Because let's face it: we mess up. Sometimes we mess up big when we do things like hate or try to hurt someone. Or when we don't respect God. Other times we mess up with lies or talking about someone or being selfish. We mess up in all kinds of different ways. Those mess-ups are called sin. And God and sin do not go together. In fact, God can't be anywhere near sin. That means our sins keep us separated from God. He doesn't want that— God wants us to be close to him! So he offers to give us grace to bring us back to him.

How can you get God's grace? That's easy. Grace is God's gift to you. It's already been bought and paid for by Jesus on the cross. All you have to do is accept it by saying, "Yes!" Say yes to believing Jesus is God's Son and that he died on the cross and was raised to life again. Say yes to loving, following, and obeying him.

IT'S YOUR TURN!

God gives you so, so much grace. When someone else messes up, be sure to give them the same love and grace that God gives to you.

17

NOTHING IS TOO HARD FOR GOD

Oh, Lord God, you made the skies and the earth with your very great power. There is nothing too hard for you to do.

JEREMIAH 32:17 NCV

The Midianites were mean and powerful. And there were a lot of them. They ate the Israelites' crops, stole their animals, and ruined their lands. Israel needed rescuing, and God chose Gideon to do it.

Gideon wasn't a soldier or a warrior. He was a farmer. But after a couple of miracles, he agreed to lead Israel's army. Gideon gathered up a huge army of Israel's soldiers—over thirty-two thousand men. But God said that was too many. "Tell anyone who is afraid to go home," God said. A lot of them were afraid. About twenty-two thousand men went home and only ten thousand stayed.

God said Gideon still had too many men. "Take them down to the water," he said. "If they lap the water up like a dog, send them home. But if they use their hands like a cup to bring the water up to their mouths, tell them to stay." Only three hundred used their hands like a cup. Everyone else went home.

Only three hundred men against thousands and thousands of trained Midianite soldiers? Impossible! Well, it might have been impossible for Gideon, and it might have been impossible for those three hundred men. But with God on their side, Gideon and his army of three hundred won.

When you feel like the odds are against you, or that there is just too much for one kid to do, remember this: You aren't alone. You have help. The things that trouble you don't trouble God. There's no problem too tough. No job too big. This is the God who created *everything* from *nothing*. There is nothing too hard for him. Just ask, and then see what he will do.

REMEMBER

Nothing is too hard for God. Trust him!

18

GOD'S STILL WORKING ON YOU

God began doing a good work in you. And he will continue it until it is finished when Jesus Christ comes again. I am sure of that.

PHILIPPIANS 1:6

Maybe you've heard of Queen Esther. She's the one who bravely went to King Xerxes and asked him to spare her people. There were feasts and scepters and plenty of death-defying moments in between. It really is a great story. (You can read all about it in the book of Esther). And Esther really was a hero who saved her people. But . . .

Did you know that at first Esther said no? That's right, Esther said no when her uncle Mordecai first asked her to help save her people. Now, don't be too hard on Esther. It was risky. No one—not even the queen—could go to the king without being called. And Esther hadn't heard from the king in weeks. Walking into the king's throne room without an invitation meant she could be killed. But with a little help from her uncle Mordecai, Esther did decide to do the right thing. And she did save her people.

The thing is, sometimes it can be hard to do the right thing. It might be a little uncomfortable. A little risky. Even a little scary. People might laugh. The other kids might not want to hang out with you. There will be times when you're like Esther, and you want to say, "Umm . . . no thanks. I'd rather not do that."

If that happens, it will be okay. God is still working on you. Talk to him. Ask him to help you know what to do and to have the courage to do it. Remember: Esther got a second chance to do the right thing. Ask God to give you one too.

God is still working on all the people around you too. So when they mess up—and they will—be ready to give them a second chance too.

PRAY

Lord, please give me the courage to do
what is right the first time. Amen.

19

WHO'S YOUR GOLIATH?

The Lord your God will go ahead of
you. He will fight for you.

DEUTERONOMY 1:30

People called Goliath a giant for a reason. He was big. Really big. Like over nine feet tall! He was also the champion fighter for the Philistines, who were the enemy of the Israelites.

The Philistine army and the Israelite army faced each other across a great valley. Every morning and every evening, Goliath marched out and shouted at the Israelites: "Choose a man and send him to fight me. If he can fight and kill me, we will become your servants. But if I defeat and kill him, you will become our servants" (1 Samuel 17:8–9). But not one Israelite soldier wanted to fight Goliath. This went on for forty days.

Then David, a shepherd boy, came to bring food to his brothers in the army. He heard Goliath's challenge and decided he would fight the giant. His brothers thought David was making fun of them. The king thought he was crazy. Goliath thought he was a joke.

But David knew something that his brothers, the king, and Goliath didn't know. David would not be the one doing the real fighting. God would be fighting for him. So David took his sling and grabbed up five smooth stones from a stream. Then he walked out to meet Goliath.

Goliath was disgusted. Who did this boy think he was? Goliath raised his sword. David slipped a stone in his sling and slung it. The stone hit Goliath. He went down. And that was the end of Goliath. Then the Israelite army chased down and defeated the Philistines.

All because David knew that God would do the fighting for him.

Who is your Goliath? Is he or she a giant of a bully who marches through the halls of school? Or that kid in your neighborhood who's always laughing at you? Or maybe your Goliath isn't a *who*. It's a *what*—like speaking in front of the whole class or trying something new. Whoever or whatever your "Goliath" is, remember this: God will do the fighting for you too.

IT'S YOUR TURN!

Is there a Goliath-sized problem that's bothering you? Talk to God about it, then look for ways that he's already fighting for you.

20

"THOUGHT" PLANES

We capture every thought and make
it give up and obey Christ.

2 CORINTHIANS 10:5

There are a lot of things we don't get to choose. We don't get to choose whether it will rain. Or what time it gets dark. Or how much salt is in the ocean or how many stars are up in the sky.

When you're a kid, it seems like there are even more things you don't get to choose. Like where you live, whether you get an allowance, or what time is bedtime.

The fact is, no matter how old we are, there are a lot of things in life that we don't have a choice about. But there's one very important thing we all get to choose. And that is *what we think about.*

Imagine an airport. Dozens and dozens of planes circle all around, wanting to land. But each plane can only land if it gets the okay from the airport. If it doesn't get the okay, it has to fly away.

Now, think of your brain as being like that airport. Dozens and dozens of "thought" planes circle around, wanting to land. Some are thoughts about everyday things, like what shirt you should wear and what's the answer to problem number four in your homework. Other thoughts are about good things, like wondering how you can help your dad, wanting to call your grandparents, or trying to memorize a Bible verse. But other thoughts are about not-so-great things or even bad things, like how angry you are at someone, how you can get even with that bully from lunch, or how you can watch that movie without your parents finding out.

All those thoughts zoom around, but you get to choose which ones you allow to land. Which ones are you going to spend time thinking about? Make sure that the thoughts you let land are good ones. Choose to think about things that are true and right and beautiful (Philippians 4:8). If a bad thought tries to swoop in for a landing—and it will try!—just make sure it keeps zooming on by.

PRAY

Lord, please protect my thoughts. Fill my mind
with things that are good and true—like how
much I am loved and blessed by you. Amen.

21

ON THE INSIDE

*"People look at the outside of a person,
but the Lord looks at the heart."*

1 SAMUEL 16:7

A pigeonhole is just what you would expect it to be: a hole where pigeons make their nest. So if you happen to see a pigeonhole, what do you think would be inside? A pigeon, of course! And what do you think would be inside an anthill? Ants! Not koala bears, monkeys, or hippopotamuses hanging out in there.

There are some things that you can look on the outside and know what's inside. Like pigeonholes. But people are not like pigeonholes. The outside of a person might be very different from the inside. That's a lesson Samuel the prophet learned.

God sent Samuel to the town of Bethlehem to find a man named Jesse. Jesse had a whole bunch of sons, and God was going to choose one of them to be the new king of Israel. Samuel saw the oldest son,

Eliab, first. He was tall and handsome, and Samuel thought he *looked* like a king. But God said, "I have not chosen him. God does not see the same way people see. People look at the outside of a person, but the Lord looks at the heart" (1 Samuel 16:7).

One by one, Samuel looked at seven of Jesse's sons. And one by one, God said no to each of them. "Are these all the sons you have?" Samuel asked Jesse (v. 11). There was just one more. Jesse sent for David, the youngest son, who was out in the fields. This time God said, "He is the one" (v. 12). Why? Because God knew David would do the things he wanted him to do (Acts 13:22).

When you meet someone, don't look at their clothes, their hair, or the color of their skin. Don't decide they must be a nerd, or supercool. Give them a chance. Get to know them. Find out what they think, what makes them laugh, and what they like—and don't like—to do. Find out who they are on the inside. Where it really counts. Because people are not like pigeonholes.

PRAY

God, help me to care about what is inside a person,
not what they look like on the outside. Amen.

22

GOD IS STILL GOD

When all that is good falls apart, what can good people do?

PSALM 11:3

My favorite part of the Bible to read is . . . well, honestly, it's whatever I'm reading at the moment. I read a lot in the book of Psalms, though, so it's definitely one of my favorite parts.

One reason I love Psalms is because King David wrote a whole bunch of them. When you read his psalms, you can tell he was a real, live person. And he wasn't afraid to be honest with God.

King David talked to God about everything. He told God about his worries and fears. He told him about the things that made him happy and sad. David even talked about his enemies and the times he was angry. King David also asked God lots of questions, like this one: "When all that is good falls apart, what can good people do?"

Because sometimes it might seem like everything *is* falling apart. If you look around at the world, there's some pretty big stuff that's going wrong. There are wars and fighting. There are diseases and viruses. People are saying that right things are bad and wrong things are good. And people are hating each other because of what they look like or where they come from.

All this stuff has been happening since Adam and Eve first took a bite of that forbidden fruit. A couple of thousand years ago, Jesus warned us, "In this world you will have trouble." But he also said, "Be brave! I have defeated the world!" (John 16:33).

There's no doubt that you need to be brave in this world. But you *can* be brave because no matter what kind of craziness happens, God is still God. He is still on his throne (Psalm 11:4). He is still in control (Proverbs 19:21). And he is still going to keep his promise to take care of you (Psalm 55:22).

IT'S YOUR TURN!

Start a collection! Grab a notebook and start
a collection of your favorite Bible verses and
stories. Add pictures, stickers, notes about why
each one is a favorite, or whatever you want!

23

GOD LISTENS!

When a believing person prays, great things happen.

JAMES 5:16 NCV

What happens when you pray? God listens! That's right! The God who made the oceans wave, the eagles soar, and the lions roar listens to what you have to say.

The second you start speaking, God starts listening. There's no delay. No "wait a minute" or "hang on a second."

Want proof that God listens? Let's take a look at the story of Elijah. He was a prophet of God who lived under the rule of the evilest of all the evil kings: King Ahab. It was a bad time for God's people. Not only were their leaders all evil, but many, many people had started worshiping this phony god they called Baal. Then along came Elijah.

Elijah challenged 450 of Baal's prophets to a sort of duel. Each side would build an altar of wood and stone. Next, they would each sacrifice a bull and put it on top. Then Elijah said, "You prophets of

Baal, pray to your god. And I will pray to the Lord. The god who answers the prayer will set fire to his wood. He is the true God" (1 Kings 18:24).

The prophets of Baal prayed all afternoon. They danced. They shouted. They whirled around. But nothing happened. At last, Elijah said, "My turn." He rebuilt the altar that Baal's guys had knocked down with all their dancing. To make the challenge a little more interesting, Elijah soaked the altar with water—so much water that it ran off the sides. Then Elijah prayed, and God answered *immediately*. Fire shot down and burned up everything—even the stones! When the people saw this, they fell to the ground and worshiped God.

God loved hearing Elijah's prayer. He loves hearing your prayers too. Why? Because just like Elijah, you are his child—and he loves to hear from you.

REMEMBER

Your prayers are important to God
because *you* are important to God.

24

THE LORD'S ARMY

God is our refuge and strength, always
ready to help in times of trouble.

PSALM 46:1 NLT

God is always near us. Always with us. Always for us. We might forget about him, but he never forgets about us—not for one single second. He fights for us. And even though we may not see them, when we're in trouble, God sends his armies to surround and protect us.

One man actually got to see those heavenly armies. He was the servant of Elisha, who was a prophet of God. A prophet is a person who says things inspired by God. In those days, the Israelites were at war with the king of Aram and his armies. With God's help, Elisha always seemed to know when Aram's army was going to strike. He would warn the Israelites, and they would be saved.

The king of Aram was not happy about this. He sent a large army in the night to capture Elisha. When Elisha's servant woke the next morning, he saw that they were surrounded by the enemy. But Elisha told him, "Don't be afraid. The army that fights for us is larger than the one against us" (2 Kings 6:16). Then Elisha prayed for the Lord to open the servant's eyes.

The Lord did open that servant's eyes. And he saw that the hills all around them were filled with horses and chariots of fire. It was the Lord's army! Just imagine how amazing that would be to see!

The enemy didn't capture Elisha or his servant that day. In fact, with God's help, Elisha captured their entire army! Because when it comes to protecting his people, God doesn't mess around.

There may be days when you feel like you're surrounded by the enemy—when your troubles are just too big or too many. Remember that servant and the army of the Lord he saw that day. And know that the army that fights for you is bigger than the one that is against you.

IT'S YOUR TURN!

What do you think that heavenly army looked like? Draw a picture of God's heavenly army surrounding you.

25

NOT YOUR BATTLE

The battle is not your battle. It is God's battle.

2 CHRONICLES 20:15

The army of Moab was coming. They were huge. They were mighty. And they scared King Jehoshaphat. So he did what any good king who loved God would do. He gathered the people together. All the men, women, babies, and children. They all prayed together, praising God and asking him to help them.

The Lord gave his people an answer that day through the prophet Jahaziel. "Don't be afraid or discouraged because of this large army. The battle is not your battle. It is God's battle," Jahaziel said. "Tomorrow go down there. . . . You won't need to fight in this battle. Just stand strong in your places. You will see the Lord save you. . . . Don't be afraid. Don't be discouraged. The Lord is with you. So go out against those people tomorrow!" (2 Chronicles 20:15–17).

King Jehoshaphat and all the people bowed down and worshiped the Lord. Then Jehoshaphat's army got ready to face the enemy. But first, Jehoshaphat switched things up a little. Instead of putting his best and bravest soldiers at the front of the army, he chose some men to be singers and put *them* at the front. They led the army out to battle, praising the Lord the whole way. But when they got there, the Lord had already defeated the army of Moab. Not one soldier was left. So Jehoshaphat led the army back to Jerusalem, and they praised God the whole way.

Deciding to follow God doesn't mean you'll never have another problem. Trouble is still going to come your way. Sometimes that trouble might get pretty big. There may be times when you'll wonder how you'll ever fight your way through. But you don't have to. Ask God to help you. And then face that problem singing God's praises the whole way through. Because God will fight for you.

PRAY

God, I praise you for the way you fight for me. I know there's no trouble bigger or stronger than you. Amen.

26

WHEN YOU'RE FACING LIONS

*"You will call my name. You will come to me
and pray to me. And I will listen to you."*

JEREMIAH 29:12

Daniel worked as an official in King Darius's government. He did such a good job that King Darius planned to put him in charge of all the other officials. The other officials didn't like that idea. So they set a trap for Daniel.

Those evil officials knew that Daniel prayed to God three times a day. So they tricked King Darius into making a law that said people could pray only to the king. Lawbreakers would be thrown into a den of lions. King Darius liked the idea of people praying to him, so he signed the law. And once it was signed, it couldn't be changed. Not even by the king.

When Daniel heard about the law, he went to his house, kneeled down by his window, and prayed. Just as he did every day. The Bible says that Daniel thanked God. But I'm guessing he also said a few words like, "Could you keep me out of that lions' den, Lord?"

Of course, the evil officials spotted Daniel praying. Daniel was arrested, and before he could say, "Hey, I'm allergic to lions," he was tossed in the den with them.

King Darius was very upset, and he called out, "May the God you serve all the time save you!" (Daniel 6:16). That was right before Daniel was sealed inside with the lions. All night long.

The good news is that God sent an angel to shut the lions' mouths and keep Daniel safe. But why didn't God save Daniel sooner? I think it's because of what happened the next morning. Darius ran to check on Daniel. When he found his friend safe and sound, Darius praised God. He even wrote a letter telling his whole kingdom how awesome God was. That wouldn't have happened if Daniel hadn't been thrown in that den.

If God doesn't answer your prayers right away, it doesn't mean he didn't hear you. It might just be because he wants someone else to see him.

REMEMBER

When you pray, God hears you! When you
pray, God listens to every word.

27

HEAVENLY HELPERS

He has put his angels in charge of you. They
will watch over you wherever you go.

PSALM 91:11

Way back in the Old Testament times, there was a king in Babylon named Nebuchadnezzar. He had a statue made of gold that was *ninety* feet high! King Nebuchadnezzar ordered everyone to bow down and worship the statue. Anyone who didn't would be tossed into a furnace of fire.

So . . . everyone bowed down and worshiped that statue. Well, not everyone. Shadrach, Meshach, and Abednego did not. These three guys were Israelites. Even though they had been taken as captives from their home years before, they still followed God. And they wouldn't worship anyone or anything except God.

Nebuchadnezzar was furious. He told his men to heat the furnace up even hotter than before. Then he ordered Shadrach, Meshach, and

Abednego to be tied up and thrown in. But when he looked into the furnace, Nebuchadnezzar saw *four* men walking around in the flames!

"Come out!" the king called to Shadrach, Meshach, and Abednego (Daniel 3:26).

Shadrach, Meshach, and Abednego stepped out of the flames. They were not hurt at all. They didn't even smell like smoke. And that fourth man? He disappeared. He was an angel who had been sent by God to save them from the fire.

That all happened long ago. But I know for a fact that angels still come and help God's people.

How do I know? Because one Sunday, after church, something amazing happened. I had just finished preaching a sermon when a lady came up to me. Her eyes were filled with wonder. She said, "I saw your angel."

"You did?" I asked.

"Yes," she said. "He stood near you as you preached."

Angels still come and help God's people. Yes, even you and me.

PRAY

Thank you, God, for sending your angels
to keep watch over me! Amen.

28

WATCH YOUR
I'S AND MY'S

Every good action and every perfect gift is from God.

JAMES 1:17

K ing Nebuchadnezzar was a great and mighty king. The problem was, he knew it.

One day, the king was out walking along the roof of his palace. As he looked out, he could see all the houses, palaces, and gardens of the city of Babylon. And he said, "I built this great city. It is my palace. I built this great place by my power to show how great I am" (Daniel 4:30).

Look at all those I's and my's! Nebuchadnezzar took all the credit for himself and didn't give one word of thanks to God.

At that very moment a voice called out from heaven: "King Nebuchadnezzar, . . . your royal power has been taken away from you. You will be forced away from people. You will live with the wild animals. You will be fed grass like an ox. Seven years will pass before you learn this lesson: The Most High God rules over the kingdoms of men" (Daniel 4:31–32).

So Nebuchadnezzar lived like an animal for seven years. He ate grass and slept in the fields. His hair grew as long as an eagle's feathers, and his nails were like claws. When at last God brought him back to his senses, Nebuchadnezzar looked up toward heaven and praised God.

It's tempting to take credit for the good grades, the winning basket, or for just how generally awesome you are. But it's important to remember that every good thing you have is a gift from God. He's the one who gave you the ability to think, who created that arm to shoot the winning shot, and who gave you all your awesomeness. So watch your I's and my's. Thank God because he's the truly awesome and amazing one.

REMEMBER

Every good thing in your life is God's gift to you.

29

JUST LIKE YOU

Our high priest [Jesus] is able to understand our weaknesses.

HEBREWS 4:15

Jesus' friend John wrote, "Before the world began, there was the Word. The Word was with God, and the Word was God. He was with God in the beginning. All things were made through him" (John 1:1–3).

If that seems a little confusing, don't worry. Let's figure it out together. "The Word" is another way of saying "Jesus." You could also say: *Before the world began, there was Jesus. Jesus was with God and Jesus was God. Jesus was with God in the beginning. All things were made through Jesus.*

Jesus was fully God.

When God said, "Let there be light!" on the first day of creation, Jesus was there (Genesis 1:3). When God breathed life into the first man, Jesus was there.

Then God sent Jesus to earth to save his people. But God didn't send Jesus as a soldier, a king, or a rich man. Jesus was born just like all babies are born. He grew up just like you and me. Like every other toddler, Jesus learned to walk and talk and get dressed all by himself. He had to figure out how to get along with his brothers and sisters when they didn't agree. There was homework to do and chores to finish before he could go outside to play. Jesus scraped his elbows and skinned his knees. He got his good clothes all dirty, and he probably smashed his finger a time or two in Joseph's workshop. Jesus got tired and hungry, angry and sad, frustrated and afraid.

Jesus was also fully human.

So if you ever wonder if Jesus understands that it's hard to get along with brothers and sisters, he does. If you ever wonder if he listens to your prayers, your stories about school, and your worries about fitting in, he does. And if you ever wonder if the one who hung the stars understands how it feels to hang your head in sadness or fear, he does. Because he was once human—just like you.

REMEMBER

Jesus became human so we know he can
understand what it's like to be you.

30

GOD CAN USE YOU

*Mary said, "My soul praises the Lord; my heart
is happy because God is my Savior."*

LUKE 1:46–47

Mary wasn't a religious leader. She wasn't the head of this or in charge of that. She wasn't rich or famous. Mary was simply Mary. She was young and poor. And she lived in Nazareth, a dusty village that everyone looked down on.

Because she was a Jew, the Romans ruled over her. Because she was a girl living in Bible times, she didn't have the best education. Because she was young, the older women always came first. And because she was poor, the rich thought they were better than her.

In other words, Mary was as ordinary as you can get.

Why would God choose her to be the mother of his Son? Because Mary's heart was not ordinary.

When the angel came and told Mary that she would be the mother of Jesus, she knew everything in her life would change. And those changes would be hard on her. But Mary didn't sputter or stutter. She didn't say, "Thanks for asking, Lord, but I'd rather not." She didn't ask, "Are you sure you have the right girl for this?" or "Wouldn't Chloe be a better choice?" No, Mary didn't say any of those things. But look at what she did say: "I am the servant girl of the Lord. Let this happen to me as you say!" (Luke 1:38).

Then Mary praised the Lord for giving her the chance to be part of his plan. And *that* is why God chose Mary.

God wants to use you in his plans too. You don't have to be perfect or popular. You don't have to be an important leader or speaker. You don't have to be rich or famous. You don't have to have it all figured out. In fact, you don't have to be any of the things that the world says are important. You just need a heart like Mary's—a heart that is willing to say, "I am your servant, Lord. Let everything happen to me just as you say!"

PRAY

Lord, I am your servant! What can
I do for you today? Amen.

31

WHAT *JESUS* MEANS

Jesus came to take away our sins.

1 JOHN 3:5 NLT

J oseph was a carpenter, and he was engaged to Mary. But before the wedding, Mary learned that she was going to have a baby. That baby was God's own Son. But Joseph didn't know that. He didn't want to embarrass Mary, so he decided that he would end their engagement quietly.

While Joseph was still thinking about how to do this, an angel of the Lord visited him in a dream. "Don't be afraid to take Mary as your wife," the angel said. "The baby in her is from the Holy Spirit. She will give birth to a son. You will name the son Jesus. Give him that name because he will save his people from their sins" (Matthew 1:20–21).

When an angel shows up in a dream with a message from God, you should probably listen. But that message to Joseph was about more than marrying Mary. It was about who that baby really was. You see, in the Hebrew language there is a special connection between the name *Jesus* and the words "save his people from their sins." Since not many of us speak Hebrew, it's easy for us to miss. But Joseph would have understood that the name *Jesus* comes from the Hebrew word *Yeshua*. And *Yeshua* is short for *Yehoshuah*, which means "Yahweh saves."[1] *Yahweh* is another way to say God.

In other words, *Jesus* means "God saves." But that's more than just his name. It's what he came to do—save his people. It's what he did on the cross—saved his people. And it's what he is still doing today—saving his people. Jesus is God saving us from our sins.

So Joseph did exactly what that angel said.

PRAY

God, thank you, thank you, and thank you again
for sending Jesus to save me from sin. Amen.

32

WHY JESUS CAME

We know that in everything God works
for the good of those who love him.

ROMANS 8:28

When the angel came to Mary and told her she would be the mother of the Son of God, Mary knew there would be many changes in her life. And there were! But God used every one of them to weave together the perfect story of his Son. Not one thing that happened was an accident. And not one moment was wasted. Just look at how Jesus came to be born in Bethlehem.

The prophets of long ago had said that the Son of God would be born in Bethlehem. But Mary and Joseph lived in Nazareth. That was sixty-five miles from Bethlehem! Today, we could hop in the car and travel that far in just an hour or so. But in Bible times, it would have taken several days to walk that far. Mary and Joseph had no reason to travel all the way to Bethlehem. At least not until the king ordered all the people to return to their hometowns to be counted. And guess where Joseph's hometown was? That's right—Bethlehem.

Joseph and Mary were forced to leave Nazareth. Jesus was born in Bethlehem. And the prophets' words came true. Because God worked to carry out his great plan. Everything that had happened led to that moment in Bethlehem.

God uses all the things that happen in our lives—the good, the bad, and all the stuff in between. He uses them all to carry out his great plan for this world and for our good. The way he does this is miraculous and wonderful. And it's something only God can do. He does it for me and for you and for everyone who chooses to follow him.

IT'S YOUR TURN!

Have you ever wished you could ask Mary and Joseph a question or two? Like, *What was it like to talk to an angel? Did Jesus ever make a mess or get into trouble? What was his favorite food?* When your family gathers around the dinner table, take turns sharing questions you wish you could ask.

33

ARE YOU MISSING SOMETHING?

"When you search for me with all your heart, you will find me!"

JEREMIAH 29:13

Mary and Joseph had traveled a long way to get to Bethlehem. It had taken days. They were both tired. And they were both ready for a soft bed and a warm meal. Especially Mary, who was about to have a baby.

But by the time they arrived in the small village, the innkeeper said all the rooms were full. There was no room left for them.

Mary and Joseph did find a place to sleep. It was with the animals, but it was warm and safe and dry. Jesus was born there that night. And he didn't seem to mind that his first bed was where the animals usually ate their breakfast. Everything worked out just as God had planned.

Do you ever wonder about that innkeeper, though? I do. I wonder if the angels woke him up later that night as they filled the skies with light and song. I wonder what he thought when a bunch of rough and ragged shepherds went running past on their way to see the Savior. And I wonder what he thought when they went running back out to the fields again, praising God every step of the way.

I wonder if that innkeeper ever knew that he had missed Jesus.

Lots of us still miss him today. We get too busy and forget about him. Or we start to think we don't need him because we can take care of ourselves. Thankfully, Jesus doesn't forget about us when we forget about him. And the fact is that we all need Jesus. No matter how grown-up we get or how good we are at taking care of ourselves.

Jesus is always with us and always working in our lives. And if you look for him, he's impossible to miss.

REMEMBER

Make sure you don't miss Jesus! Take time
to think about him every day.

34

THE GIFT YOU GIVE TO GOD

*Our Lord and God! You are worthy to receive glory
and honor and power. You made all things.*

REVELATION 4:11

When babies are born, people often give gifts. So when Jesus was born in that Bethlehem stable, there were gifts for him too. The shepherds heard about him and came running. They gave him the gift of believing in him. The wise men arrived, and—even though they were running a couple of years late—they gave Jesus gifts of gold, frankincense, and myrrh. But the angels gave Jesus a different sort of gift that night.

They filled the night sky and sang: "Give glory to God in heaven, and on earth let there be peace to the people who please God" (Luke 2:14).

The angels worshiped him. That's it. That's all they gave Jesus. Mary could've used a bed. Joseph probably would have liked a sandwich. And Baby Jesus was sleeping in a feeding trough. Why didn't the angels bring a more useful gift? After all, they were angels! Didn't they know better?

Or maybe . . . the angels knew best of all. Remember, Jesus had just come from heaven. The angels had been hanging out with him for a long time. And that's how they knew that worship is the most wonderful gift we can give to God.

What exactly is worship? It's telling God that you know who he is—the all-powerful, all-knowing God of everything. It's thanking him for all the ways he works in your life. And it's declaring that you trust him to be the Lord of your life.

Worship can happen anywhere, not just in church. It can happen on the way to school or walking down the street. You can worship first thing in the morning or as you fall asleep. You can worship with friends, with family, or when you're alone with God.

God gives you so many gifts. Worship is the gift you can give to him.

IT'S YOUR TURN!

Give Jesus the gift the angels gave him. Worship him with your words, with a song, with a poem or drawing. Tell him how wonderful you know he is!

35

FOLLOWING A STAR

When the wise men saw the star, they were filled with joy.

MATTHEW 2:10

T*he wise men.* Sometimes they're called the magi. People usually say that there were three of them because they brought three gifts: gold, frankincense, and myrrh. But we don't really know how many wise men there were.

In fact, we don't know a whole lot about the wise men themselves. Except that they were wise, and they came from an eastern land far away from Bethlehem. These men came because they saw a special star in the sky. They knew that star would lead them to the baby who was born to be the King of the Jews. So they loaded up their camels and strapped on their traveling sandals. And they followed that star all the way to Jerusalem.

In Jerusalem, the wise men went to see King Herod. (Herod was an evil, wicked king, but the wise men did not know that.) They told him who they were looking for. Herod called in the religious leaders and teachers. He asked them what the prophets said about the Christ child and where he would be born. "Bethlehem, the scriptures say," they said. Herod sent the wise men on their way. "When you find the child," he said, "come back and tell me. I want to go and worship him too."

The wise men traveled to Bethlehem. And there they found Jesus, just as the Scriptures had said. They worshiped. They gave him their gifts. But they did not go back to Herod because God had warned them about him.

God used that bright star to get the wise men's attention. It led them to Jerusalem and to the ones who knew what the Scriptures said. But God used the Scriptures—his Word—to lead them to Jesus.

God still uses his creation to get our attention. A beautiful sunset, the endless ocean, or even the simplest wildflower—they can all make us wonder who created such wonderful and amazing things. And when we look in God's Word for the answers, we find Jesus.

PRAY

God, when I look around at everything you have made, I can see how wonderful you are. You are amazing! Amen.

36

WHAT JESUS GAVE UP

[Jesus] gave up his place with God and made himself
nothing. He was born as a man and became like a servant.

PHILIPPIANS 2:7

S*acrifice* is a big word. It has an even bigger meaning. Sacrifice means giving up something very important to you in order to help someone else. Sacrifice is what Jesus did for us.

We usually think of the cross as being the sacrifice Jesus gave for us. But that wasn't the only one. There were more.

Jesus was God's one and only Son. God loved his Son with a love that was bigger than the whole universe and all its stars. It was a sacrifice for God to send his Son to save us.

And it was a sacrifice for Jesus to come. Just think: he left heaven to come here. In heaven there are no tears. Here, there are plenty of tears. In heaven there is no sickness. There is sickness everywhere on earth. In heaven there is no sadness, no unhappiness of any kind.

In a way that's so very hard to understand, he was completely God. Completely all-powerful. All the earth was created through him. He wasn't just powerful—he was really powerful. And he became a baby. He sacrificed all the perfection and power of heaven to be born as a baby who couldn't even sit up by himself.

Jesus lived on this earth—with all its sin and sadness and sickness—for thirty-three years. There's no sin in heaven, no sadness, and no sickness. In heaven, Jesus never worried about banging his thumb with a hammer in Joseph's shop. He never worried about tripping and face-planting in the dirt.

But he allowed himself to become fully human. So he had to deal with dirt and cold and hunger. He got tired and banged his knee.

We think of Jesus' sacrifice as dying on the cross. And it was. That was a terrible sacrifice. But Jesus' sacrifice actually started the moment he stepped out of heaven.

IT'S YOUR TURN!

Have you ever thought about all that Jesus gave up to come to earth and save you? Make a list—with words or pictures. Now, what can you give up for him?

37

GROWING UP
LIKE JESUS

Jesus continued to learn more and more and to grow physically. People liked him, and he pleased God.

LUKE 2:52

As you might know, growing up isn't always the easiest thing to do. There are so, so many things to learn and figure out. It sometimes seems that as soon as you figure one thing out, there's something new for you to learn. *Hooray! You've learned addition; now let's do subtraction, multiplication, and division. Hooray! You can spell* cat. *Now let's learn* moustache.

Jesus grew up too. Yes, he was the Son of God. But remember, he came to earth as a newborn baby. He had to learn all the same things you do. Check out what the Bible says about how he grew up: "Jesus continued to learn more and more and to grow physically. People liked him, and he pleased God."

Growing up isn't just about learning math and spelling words. And it isn't just about getting bigger and taller and stronger. It's also about learning how to get along with others and how to be more and more like Jesus. Those are things that really please God.

Maybe you're thinking, *How do I do all that? I'm just a kid, remember?* Well, the getting bigger and taller and stronger takes care of itself. The math and spelling will come with a little work and practice. The getting along with others and being more like Jesus—well, that's where Jesus comes in. He came to earth to be your example and to show you how to live and love the way God wants you to.

Look at all the things Jesus did and try to do them. I don't mean the miracles, of course. Only Jesus can walk on water or stop a storm. But look at the everyday things he did. Jesus prayed to his Father. He studied God's Word. He was kind and cared about others. And he helped and served others everywhere he went.

Those are all things you can do too. And when you do, you will be growing up like Jesus.

REMEMBER

Jesus came to show us how to live.

38

REMEMBER ANDREW?

The first thing Andrew did was to find his brother, Simon.
He said to Simon, "We have found the Messiah." ("Messiah"
means "Christ.") Then Andrew took Simon to Jesus.

JOHN 1:41–42

If you look at preachers like me, you might think that God's servants are pretty noisy. And that we spend a whole lot of time talking. But God's servants come in all shapes, sizes, ages . . . and noise levels.

Some are like Peter—big and bold and loud and ready to tell the whole world about Jesus. Others are more like Andrew. He was Peter's brother. Andrew's name was never at the top of the list of leaders—not like Peter, or James, or John. But he was an *amazing* servant for God. Just in his own quiet way.

Quiet doesn't mean silent, though. It doesn't mean Andrew never spoke or never did anything for Jesus. And it definitely doesn't mean unimportant. Let's just look at what we know Andrew did:

- Andrew brought Peter to meet Jesus. And then Peter went on to lead the church. He preached the gospel to thousands and thousands of people. Peter was big and bold and loud for Jesus. But without Andrew, Peter might not have met Jesus.
- When Jesus was choosing his first disciples, he stopped by Andrew and Peter's fishing boat and said, "Follow me" (Matthew 4:19). Andrew dropped his nets and followed Jesus. He didn't stop to think about it. He just followed.
- Andrew encouraged a little boy to give his lunch to Jesus. Jesus used that same lunch to feed thousands and thousands of people (Matthew 14).

I'm quite certain Andrew did many, many, many more things for Jesus. We just don't know about them. But Jesus does—and that's what really counts.

Now, maybe you're big and bold and a bit loud—and ready to tell the whole world about Jesus, like Peter did. Or maybe you're more like Andrew. And you quietly do whatever you can do to serve Jesus. Either way, Jesus sees what you do, and he loves you.

IT'S YOUR TURN!

Even big and bold servants need to be quiet
sometimes. Practice being like Andrew. Help
someone without them seeing you.

39

DON'T BE "THUNDER KID"!

If someone does wrong to you, do not pay him back by doing wrong to him. Try to do what everyone thinks is right.

ROMANS 12:17

Do you have nickname? Lots of people do. Nicknames tell us something about a person. For example, someone called "Red" probably has red hair. "Sunny" might smile a lot, while "Doc" is really, really smart.

So what would you think of a couple of guys who were nicknamed the "Sons of Thunder"? You might think they would have a little bit of a temper, right? And they did! Like a big, booming thunderstorm. Who were these guys? James and John. That's right! They were two of Jesus' closest disciples. And he's the one who gave them their Sons of Thunder nickname (Mark 3:17).

Too often, James and John would let their anger take over. Like the time Jesus wanted to stay in a Samaritan village. But because he was a Jew, the Samaritan people there didn't want him around. When James and John saw this, they were furious. "Lord," they asked, "do you want us to call fire down from heaven to destroy those people?" (Luke 9:54).

Ouch! Talk about Sons of Thunder!

But Jesus scolded them. He didn't come to destroy people. Jesus came to save them!

Now, before we think too badly about James and John, how many times have we done the same thing? Oh, maybe we haven't called down fire from heaven. But we've let fiery words shoot out of our mouths. Or we've let our hot tempers take over and tried to get even with someone who has hurt us. That's not what Jesus wants us to do!

Jesus wants us to do this instead: Don't shoot out fiery words and don't fight with your fists (Matthew 5:39). Instead of more evil, let's give more kindness (Romans 12:14). Pray good things for your enemies, not bad (v. 17).

Live so that no one ever calls you "Thunder Kid."

PRAY

God, it's not easy to pay back evil with kindness.
I'm going to need your help. Thank you for
helping me to do what is right. Amen.

40

SQUARE BLOCKS

Christ accepted you, so you should accept each
other. This will bring glory to God.

ROMANS 15:7

When you were little, did you have one of those toys where you put different-shaped blocks into the matching holes? Do you remember what happened when you tried to put the square block in the round hole? It didn't fit, did it? All those sharp square corners would not go through those round curves.

Some people are kind of like those square blocks. They're a little sharp around the edges. And they don't seem to fit with everyone else.

Matthew—who was also called Levi—was a square block. The Romans didn't like him because he was a Jew. And the Jews didn't like him because he collected taxes for the Romans. He didn't fit in anywhere—at least not until Jesus came along. Jesus spotted Matthew sitting in his tax collector's office and said, "Follow me!" (Luke 5:27).

Matthew immediately jumped up, left everything behind, and followed Jesus. Matthew became one of Jesus' twelve closest disciples. And later, he wrote the book of Matthew, telling the world all about the one who reached out and invited him in.

Do you have any Matthews in your world? Any square blocks that just don't fit in? These are the people who are the opposite of you. They can drive you a little crazy and get on your last nerve. Maybe it's the neighbor whose dog just loves to chase your cat. Or the sister who never wants to watch the show you want to watch. Maybe it's a teacher or a kid at school. But no matter what, you just can't seem to agree.

What do you do with people like these? Accept them. And try to be a friend. That's what Jesus did.

IT'S YOUR TURN!

Do you know any square blocks, any Matthews?
Decide to pray for them each day. Ask Jesus to
help you invite them to get to know him.

41

GAME OVER

The Son of God came to destroy the works of the devil.

1 JOHN 3:8 NLT

When Jesus began his work here on the earth, Satan knew that could *not* be good for him. So he set out to trick and trap Jesus.

God knew what Satan was up to, and his Spirit led Jesus into the desert for the showdown. First, Jesus fasted for forty days—he didn't eat a thing. At the end of those forty days, He was hungry. *Really hungry.* That's when Satan showed up and said, "If you are the Son of God, tell these rocks to become bread" (Matthew 4:3).

Imagine how wonderful bread would taste after forty days of nothing to eat! Jesus didn't come to serve himself, though. He came to serve others (20:28). Jesus used God's own words to break free from that trap: "A person does not live only by eating bread. But a person lives by everything the Lord says" (4:4).

Satan also tried to get Jesus to test God—to see if God really would keep his promises. That didn't work either. Next, he tempted Jesus with all the wealth and power of the world. Again, Jesus fought Satan off by using God's Word. Satan went away, but he watched and waited for another chance to attack.

There is no doubt that Satan is real. And there is no doubt that his tricks and traps are real. But there is also no doubt that, on the cross, Jesus beat him. Satan just hasn't given up yet.

It's like being at a ball game when the score is 101 to 3 with only seconds left to play. There's no way for the losing team to come back and win. But they keep on trying until the game is over. Satan will keep on sinning, lying, and setting traps until Jesus comes back again. And then it will be "game over" for him.

PRAY

God, open my eyes to see all the tricks and traps of Satan—and help me to stay far away from him. Amen.

42

STUFF YOU
SHOULD KNOW

*God is the one who saves me; I will
trust him and not be afraid.*

ISAIAH 12:2 NCV

There are some pretty important things that you need to know when you live in this world. Things like looking both ways before you cross the street, knowing who to call in an emergency, and knowing just exactly how long you can leave your cookie dunked in the milk before it falls to pieces.

A kid—even a grown-up one like me—needs to know this kind of stuff!

Of course, there are lots of other things you need to know too. But the most important things are the ones God wants you to know. These matter even more than the cookies and milk thing. Yep, they're that important. Things like, God won't ever leave you all alone. He is always ready to help you. And you are stronger than you think because God is closer than you think.

Here are a few more things God wants you to know:

- He knows when you sit down, when you get up, when you climb up in a tree, and when you blow bubbles with your favorite gum (Psalm 139:2).
- He knows exactly how many hairs you have on your head—and how many you lost that time you cut your own hair when you were two (Matthew 10:29–31).
- He loves you just as he loves Jesus (1 John 3:1).
- He knew all about you even before you were born (Jeremiah 1:4–5).
- He will take care of you (Matthew 6:31–33).
- He loves you to infinity and back again (1 John 3:1).

Yep. Pretty important things. Now, aren't you glad you know?

IT'S YOUR TURN!

If you wanted to tell someone about Jesus—
someone who didn't know anything about him—
what would you want them to know?

43

BE BOLD

This is the boldness we have in God's presence:
that if we ask God for anything that agrees
with what he wants, he hears us.

1 JOHN 5:14 NCV

God wants to hear from you. That's right. *You!* Your prayers are important to him. And when you pray for his help, wonderful things happen. Just look at the story of a soldier and his servant.

Jesus had just arrived in the city of Capernaum. A soldier came to meet him. This was no ordinary soldier. He was a centurion—an important officer in the army in charge of many other men. The officer begged Jesus to heal his servant. The servant was in so much pain that he could not even get out of bed. Jesus said, "I will go and heal him" (Matthew 8:7).

But the centurion said, "Lord, I am not good enough for you to come into my house. All you need to do is command that my servant be healed, and he will be healed" (v. 8). You see, because the centurion was part of the Roman army, he was an enemy of the Jews. But he loved his servant so much that he dared to ask Jesus for help. The centurion also knew that Jesus could give a command and it would happen just as he said. Jesus didn't have to come to his house. "I have soldiers under my command," the centurion told Jesus. "I tell one soldier, 'Go,' and he goes. I tell another soldier, 'Come,' and he comes. I say to my servant, 'Do this,' and my servant obeys me" (v. 9).

Jesus was amazed by the centurion's faith. "Go home," he said. "Your servant will be healed just as you believed he would" (v. 13). And at that very moment the servant was healed.

When you need help, go to the one who can help you. Go to the one who can do anything. Don't be shy. Don't wait for just the right time. Be bold—and go to the God who is ready to listen and help you.

REMEMBER

You can always talk to God—anytime
and anywhere, about anything.

44

MORE THAN A
LITTLE LUNCH

*Do not forget to do good to others. And
share with them what you have.*

HEBREWS 13:16

T housands of people had gathered on a hill to hear Jesus teach.
For hours they sat and listened and learned. But it was getting
late, and stomachs were grumbling. There weren't any towns close by.
There weren't any places to grab a quick burger and fries. In fact, there
weren't any burgers and fries—no one had invented them yet!

Maybe that's why the disciples were so shocked when Jesus asked,
"Where can we buy bread for all these people to eat?" (John 6:5).

"Buy bread? For all these people? Impossible!" the disciples said.
Didn't Jesus see how many people there were? There were at least five
thousand men, plus even more women and children.

Then Andrew stepped up with a young boy carrying his lunch. It wasn't much. Just two little fish and five small loaves of bread. Not nearly enough to feed all the people. Still, Jesus took the loaves and the fish, and he thanked God for them. Then the disciples began giving the food to the people—and they never ran out! They even had leftovers!

Only Jesus could feed thousands of people with one small lunch. But look at where that miracle began. It started with a boy—probably about your age—who was willing to share what he had.

What about you? Maybe you're thinking, *I'm just a kid. I don't have much to share.* That's okay. Just share what you have. Because Jesus can take a small thing and do great big things with it. So give your pennies and dimes to the missionary. Offer a bottle of water to that homeless person. Share your lunch. Give a smile. Say a prayer.

Because the miracle isn't in you. It's not in what you have to give. The miracle is in Jesus. He can feed thousands with one kid's lunch. Just imagine what he can do with what you have.

REMEMBER

God can use little things to do big things!

45

HELP IS ON THE WAY

"You can be sure that I will be with you always."

MATTHEW 28:20

It had been a *really* long day. The disciples had lugged around baskets of fish and bread—baskets that Jesus miraculously kept filled until more than five thousand people were fed. Now it was dark, and Jesus had gone up into the hills alone.

The disciples climbed into their boat and began rowing across the Sea of Galilee. They had made it to the middle of the lake when a storm blew in. The wind howled around them. The waves splashed and crashed over the edge of their boat. It was dark. There was no land in sight. And no matter how hard they rowed, the disciples could not get to shore. They began to worry.

Then one of them shouted, "Look!" There was something moving out there in the darkness. No, it was someone! *Someone* was out there, walking on the water! How could that be possible? The disciples were not just worried anymore. They were terrified. But then the person called out, "Don't be afraid. It is I" (John 6:20). It was Jesus!

Don't you wish the Bible told us a little bit more? Like, was the water up to Jesus' ankles or just over his toes? Did his robe get wet? Did the wind dare to blow his hair? But God's Word simply says, "They saw Jesus walking on the water, coming toward the boat" (v. 19). And really, that's all we need to know. Because when the disciples saw that it was Jesus, they welcomed him into the boat. The storm stopped. And their boat quickly landed on the shore, exactly where the disciples wanted to go.

When you're worried, when you're scared, when the waves of your troubles are getting bigger than your "boat," you might start to wonder where Jesus is. Here's the answer: he's on his way to help you. Don't be afraid. Just welcome him into your boat. Because before Jesus stops the storms, he comes and joins you in the middle of them.

PRAY

Lord, when my problem seems so huge, help me remember
that you are bigger. I know you will take care of me!

46

THERE'S NO AWESOME WITHOUT GOD

The Lord is great. He is worthy of our praise.

PSALM 145:3

You're great. You're awesome. You really are. God's own Word says that you are "fearfully and wonderfully made" (Psalm 139:14 NIV). And your grandmother says so too, so you know it has to be true.

It's good to know that. There's no reason to think that you are less than wonderful. But it's also good to know that no matter how great and awesome, no matter how fearfully and wonderfully made you are—you are not God.

There's a joke I love to tell that shows how true this is:

A proud man decided that he was just as smart as God. He believed that he could do anything God could do. The man looked up into the heavens and said, "Hey, God! I can do whatever you can do. I can create a person out of dust. I know how all these cells and bones and nerves work. I can create life too!"

"All right," said God. "Let's see what you can do."

The man rubbed his hands together with excitement. Then he reached down and scooped up a handful of dirt to start shaping it into a person. But before he could do anything else, God stopped him. "I thought you said you could do what I did."

"I can," the man answered.

"Well, then," God told him, "go and get your own dirt."

Pretty funny, huh? It's pretty true too. I mean, can you make dirt? I know I can make things. I'm really good at that. But I can't make actual dirt. That's something only God can do.

Whenever you do something amazing, or whenever you're feeling just plain awesome, stop for a minute and remember who you really are. You're good, but you're not God. And there's no awesome or amazing without him.

PRAY

God, I want to praise you for how wonderful and amazing
you are. No one else can do all the things you do! Amen.

47

JESUS FINDS YOU

When people insult you because you follow Christ,
then you are blessed. You are blessed because the
glorious Spirit, the Spirit of God, is with you.

1 PETER 4:14

One day, Jesus and his followers saw a man who was born blind. Jesus spat on the ground and made some mud. He put the mud on the man's eyes—the man probably was not expecting that! Then Jesus said, "Go and wash in the Pool of Siloam" (John 9:7). The man did just as Jesus said, and he could see! For the first time in his whole life, he could see colors, buildings, and trees!

There was just one problem. Jesus healed the man on the Sabbath day, the day of rest. It wasn't a problem for Jesus. But it was a big problem for the religious leaders. They thought it was a terrible sin. They asked the man question after question about who had healed him. But the man didn't know Jesus' name. He knew only one thing: "I was blind, and now I can see" (v. 25).

The more the leaders questioned the man, the angrier they became. Finally, they got so angry that they threw the no-longer-blind man out of the synagogue. He had no one left to turn to. Not even his family and friends could help him.

Jesus heard what had happened and went to the man. And that's when Jesus helped the man see something much more wonderful than the sky or trees. He helped him see that the one who had healed his eyes was the Savior. The man bowed down and worshiped him.

When Jesus is a part of your life, you begin to change. You begin to see every moment as a chance to love and serve Jesus. So you try to be kinder and do what is right. You try to live the way Jesus wants you to. Other people don't always understand that. They might laugh or make fun of you. But don't worry, and don't stop living for him. Jesus will find you. He will comfort you and help you know how to keep following him.

PRAY

God, please open my eyes and help me see the
way you are working all around me. Amen.

48

FRIENDS CARRY FRIENDS TO JESUS

*Pray for all people. Ask God for the things
people need, and be thankful to him.*

1 TIMOTHY 2:1

The four men had just heard the news: Jesus was in town! Together, they gathered up their friend who lay on his mat. He wasn't able to walk, and the friends knew Jesus was the only one who could help him.

They hurried to the house where Jesus was staying. But it was so packed with people that they couldn't even squeeze inside. *What were they going to do?* That's when one of them had an idea: the roof! They carried their friend up and began to make a hole in the roof—right over the place where Jesus was teaching. It wasn't easy. First, they pulled away the branches that were woven together on top. Then they chipped away at the hard clay underneath. Little by little, they made a hole big enough to fit their friend through.

Slowly and carefully they lowered their friend down through the roof, down onto the floor—right in front of Jesus. He saw their great faith and knew they believed in him. So he said to the man on the mat, "Your sins are forgiven" (Mark 2:5).

This made the religious leaders very angry. "Only God can forgive sins," they said to themselves (v. 7).

That's when Jesus said, "Which is easier: to tell this paralyzed man, 'Your sins are forgiven,' or to tell him, 'Stand up. Take your mat and walk'? But I will prove to you that the Son of Man has authority on earth to forgive sins." So Jesus said to the paralyzed man, "I tell you, stand up. Take your mat and go home" (vv. 9–11). And that's exactly what the man did. All because four friends had carried their hurting friend to Jesus.

Do you carry your friends to Jesus? Not on a mat, but in prayer? Whether your friend is hurting, needs encouraging, or doesn't know Jesus, the best thing you can do is carry them to Jesus in prayer. Because he loves them even more than you do.

REMEMBER

Carry your friends to Jesus in prayer!

49

GET BUSY

"Stand up. Pick up your mat and walk."

JOHN 5:8

When you've got a problem, the first thing you should do is pray. When you're worried and afraid, that's the time to pray too. Ask God to help you. Ask him to fix your problem. And ask him to take your worries and fears away.

But after you pray, you can't just sit on the couch and play video games until God makes everything okay again. Because if you do, chances are, nothing will change. Jesus said you need to "stand up. Pick up your mat and walk" (John 5:8). Or at least that's what he said to the man waiting by the pool of Bethesda.

Crowds of sick people had gathered by the pool. They gathered there because they believed the angel of the Lord sometimes came down and stirred up the pool. The first one into the pool after that would be healed. One man had been lying there, waiting for thirty-eight years.

Jesus said to the man, "Stand up. Pick up your mat and walk." And the man did. The healing power came from Jesus, but the man had to do something too—he had to obey Jesus. What do you think would have happened if the man had not stood up or picked up his mat? He wouldn't have walked either.

If something is wrong in your world, this is what you need to do:

- *Stand up.* Do the right thing. If you hurt someone's feelings, say you're sorry. If you lied, tell the truth.
- *Pick up your mat.* Stop doing the wrong things. If a friend is always leading you into trouble, find a new friend. If a TV show puts bad words in your head, stop watching it.
- And *walk.* Get closer to God. Talk to him, pray to him, and obey him.

When you need God's help in your life, ask for it. But while you're waiting for his answer, get busy obeying him.

IT'S YOUR TURN!

Waiting is hard to do. What good things can you do while you're waiting on God to answer your prayers?

50

BECAUSE OF LOVE

God was pleased for all of himself to live in Christ.

COLOSSIANS 1:19

Life in heaven is perfect. There are no tears because no one is ever hurting or sad. There is no pain or sickness. There is no more death or darkness. There is only light, and love, and God and his Son. That's what the Bible tells us. I believe heaven will be better than anything we could ever imagine. Better than every Christmas, every birthday, and every trip to the zoo all stacked up together and rolled into one.

You need only one word to describe heaven: *perfect*. But you need two words to describe life here on earth: *not perfect*.

Here on earth, we still have tears. We still have pain and sickness and sadness. And we still have darkness and death. We also have anger, selfishness, and just plain meanness. That's not what God had in mind when he created the world. He could have just thrown up his hands and said, "I give up! There's just too much sin! I'm outta here." But he didn't. God loved us too much to leave us in the middle of this mess. So he came up with a plan. A great and wonderful plan:

God was pleased for all of himself to live in Christ.

That means that God poured all his power and strength into Jesus. He poured all his kindness into Jesus. And he poured all his love into Jesus. And then he asked Jesus to leave the perfection of heaven and come to earth to save us. And he did!

Why would Jesus do that? Why would he leave all the wonders of heaven to come to earth with all our mess-ups and sin and troubles?

Because that's how much Jesus loves us. Because that's how much Jesus loves you.

PRAY

Thank you, Jesus, for loving me so much
that you left heaven to save me. Amen.

51

KING OF THE MOUNTAIN

Do not think that you are better than you are.

ROMANS 12:3

The other day I saw some kids playing in an empty lot where someone had dumped a big mound of dirt. They were playing one of my all-time favorite kid games: King of the Mountain. The rules are really simple. They're also a bit heartless: if you want to be king, you have to push your way to the top and shove off anyone who tries to take your place. There's a whole lot of crawling, pushing, and falling in the dirt. It's great!

Okay. So maybe it's not the most peaceful game. And you definitely don't want to play it in your church clothes. But the real problem with King of the Mountain is that people don't just play it in empty lots and on dirt mounds.

All kinds of different King of the Mountain games get played out all over the place. People push and shove each other. Sometimes with their words and attitudes. Sometimes with their hands and fists.

Maybe where you are, it's King of the Playground, King of the Lunch Table, or even King of the House. The problem is there's only room for one king. Now, maybe you're thinking, *But it's good to be king. Everyone will look up to me and know that I'm special and important. That I'm the best.* Except . . . if you're going to be the king, that means everyone else has to be shoved down so that they're less important than you.

God doesn't want you to push people down. He wants you to pull them up. Say a kind word. Reach out a hand. Help others to feel good about themselves. Because acting—and even thinking—that you're better than someone else can cause hurt feelings, anger, arguments with brothers and sisters, and broken friendships.

In other words, it's not always good to be king. Help everyone else climb the mountain instead!

REMEMBER

There's only one true King of the Mountain—
the one who made the mountains!

52

WHAT'S YOUR ANSWER?

"If anyone stands before other people and says he believes in me, then I will say that he belongs to me. I will say this before my Father in heaven."

MATTHEW 10:32

If you're like me when I was a kid, you get asked a lot of questions. Things like, *Did you feed the dog? Did you finish your homework? Did you do your chores?* And then, of course, there's this question: *What do you want to be when you grow up?* You're going to be asked that a lot!

There are questions from your teacher, from your parents and grandparents, from Great-Uncle Nosy Ned. Over the years, you'll answer thousands—maybe millions—of questions. But there's one question that's more important than any other question you'll ever be asked. It's the one question everyone has to answer. And it's the same one Jesus asked Peter.

"Who do you say I am?" (Matthew 16:15).

When Jesus asked that question, he had been teaching and preaching for a while. And a lot of people were talking about him. Some were saying he was John the Baptist. Others were saying he was Elijah or one of the other great prophets come back to life. But what Jesus most wanted to know was who his disciples thought he was. After all, they were the ones closest to him, the ones he had taught the most, and the ones who knew him best. So Jesus asked, "Who do you say I am?"

It was Peter who answered. "You are the Christ, the Son of the living God," he said (v. 16).

Peter got the answer perfectly right. Because Jesus wasn't just a great man, and he wasn't just a prophet. He was—and is—the Son of God, who came to this earth to save his people.

Why is this question so important? Because Jesus promises that if you tell other people who he is, he will tell God the Father who you are—one of his.

IT'S YOUR TURN!

Ask yourself that most important question: Who do you believe Jesus is? Why do you believe that? Ask your mom and dad to help you find the answer for yourself.

53

A TRUE TONGUE TWISTER

Love one another.

1 JOHN 3:11 NIV

I love tongue twisters. You know, those funny sayings that twist your tongue all up in a knot. Like, *She sells seashells by the seashore.* Or, *How much wood would a woodchuck chuck if a woodchuck could chuck wood?* Say that ten times, real fast!

Here's another for you: *Doing good is good for the one who does good.* Except this one isn't just fun to say; it's true! It's also the way Jesus wants us to live.

The Bible tells us that "Jesus went everywhere doing good" (Acts 10:38). He is our example to follow (1 Peter 2:21). And the Bible is filled with ideas for how to be more like him. I like to call them the "One Anothers." Here are just a few:

- Encourage one another (1 Thessalonians 5:11 NIV).
- Be gentle and patient with one another (Ephesians 4:2).
- Pray for one another (James 5:16).
- Serve one another (Galatians 5:13).
- Strengthen one another (Colossians 3:16).
- Forgive one another (Ephesians 4:32).
- Love one another (1 John 3:11).

When you practice doing the "One Anothers" like Jesus did, you are doing good for others. But something wonderful happens for you too. You become a little bit more like him. And that's the beginning of the most beautiful circle in life: You do good. You become more like Jesus. Which makes you want to do more good. Which makes you more like Jesus. Which makes you . . . You get the picture, right?

Doing good is good for the one who does good. Yeah, it's a true tongue twister. And it's also the best way to live.

IT'S YOUR TURN!

Start your own "circle of goodness." Choose
a "One Another" from above. Do it today—
and see where it takes you tomorrow!

54

THE LEAST AT
THE FEAST

*"The Son of Man did not come for other people
to serve him. He came to serve others."*

MATTHEW 20:28

Simon was a religious leader. He asked Jesus to eat dinner with him one day. A woman who had done many wrong things heard that Jesus was there. She went to Simon's house and brought along a jar of expensive perfume. She knelt at Jesus' feet and began to wash them with her tears. Then she dried them with her hair, kissing them and rubbing them with the perfume.

Simon was horrified. *If Jesus really was a prophet*, he thought to himself, *he would know that this woman touching his feet is a sinner!*

Jesus knew what Simon was thinking. "When I came into your house," Jesus said, "you gave me no water for my feet. But she washed my feet with her tears and dried my feet with her hair. You did not kiss me, but she has been kissing my feet since I came in! You did not rub my head with oil, but she rubbed my feet with perfume." Then Jesus turned to the woman and said, "Your sins are forgiven" (Luke 7:44–48).

Simon had invited Jesus into his home, but he didn't offer even a drop of water for Jesus' feet. In Bible times, that was very rude. Much worse than burping or putting your elbows on the table! Simon was far too important to worry about washing feet. Yet the woman—who was the least at the feast—was grateful for the chance to serve Jesus, the Lord she loved.

You can do the same. You can serve the one who loves you. How? By serving the ones he loves. Don't be so "important" that you won't get your hands dirty. Be willing to be the "least at the feast." That's what the woman did.

IT'S YOUR TURN!

Find a job no one else wants to do and do it. Maybe it's taking out the trash, sweeping the floor, or picking up after the dog. Try not to let anyone see you—serve in secret.

55

WHEN YOU CAN'T SEE

We walk by faith, not by sight.

2 CORINTHIANS 5:7 ESV

There's a trail that goes right through the wilderness of the Appalachian Mountains. It's called the Appalachian Trail. And it's over twenty-one hundred miles long. It stretches from Georgia all the way up to Maine—going through fourteen different states! But this is no nice, paved road. It's a rough trail that climbs up and over mountains. Hikers climb so many mountains that if you added them all up, it would be like climbing up and down Mount Everest sixteen times![2]

The path is sometimes rocky, sometimes muddy, and often filled with tree roots. There are streams to cross. Oh, and there are bears and snakes. The trail is easy to follow, though. The whole thing is marked by 165,000 white blazes—or patches—painted on poles, rocks, and trees.

It's easy to follow unless you happen to be blind, like Bill Irwin. Bill and his guide dog, Orient, hiked the entire trail. He didn't use a map or a compass. Bill used 2 Corinthians 5:7 as his guide: "We walk by faith, not by sight" (esv). The hike took eight months. He prayed often and told plenty of people about Jesus along the way.[3]

Bill guessed that he fell about five thousand times along the trail. He battled the cold, cracked his ribs, and skinned his hands and knees more times than he could count. But he never stopped trusting that God would lead him the right way. He made the long walk by faith, not by sight.[4]

Life can be a lot like hiking that Appalachian Trail. There are mountains of troubles to climb over and dark forests to get through. Rocky days can trip you up. But there are also so many amazing things that happen along the way. When you can't see where you're going, trust God to lead you. Fill your days with prayers of "Help me, God." And always say "Thank you, Lord" every time he answers you.

REMEMBER

Two of the greatest prayers are "Help me,
God" and "Thank you, Lord."

56

GOD LOVES

Christ's love is greater than any person can ever know.
But I pray that you will be able to know that love.

EPHESIANS 3:19

Imagine that you are a shepherd. You've got a robe to wear and one of those big staffs with a hook on the end to carry around. And sheep. *Lots* of sheep. Actually, you've got exactly one hundred sheep to watch over. Then one day, as you're counting your sheep, you see that there are only ninety-nine out there in the meadow. One sheep is missing! What are you going to do?

That's the question Jesus asked some of the religious teachers. They were upset because Jesus was spending so much time with "sinners." (They kept forgetting that they messed up and sinned sometimes too.)

Jesus said the shepherd would leave the ninety-nine sheep and go searching for the one that was lost. The shepherd would search and search until he found it. Then he would put the sheep on his shoulders and carry it home.

The shepherd loves his sheep. And God loves you.

When you're doing everything just right, and you haven't made a mistake all day, God loves you.

When you get mad and sock your brother in the nose, God still loves you. (But don't sock your brother—or your sister—in the nose. Because Mom and Dad will still love you, but they will also ground you. Trust me on that one.)

Even when you wander away from God, and when you do things you know he doesn't want you to do, God still loves you. He even chases after you until he finds you, and then he carries you back home with him.

You can't ask a cat not to meow, a lion not to roar, a fish not to swim, or a star not to shine. And you can't ask God not to love you. Because God is love (1 John 4:8). That's who he is. And that's what he does. *God loves you.*

REMEMBER

Love is what God does.

57

DON'T WORRY; LOOK AROUND

"I tell you, don't worry about the food you need to live. And don't worry about the clothes you need for your body. Life is more important than food. And the body is more important than clothes."

MATTHEW 6:25

Jesus said, "Don't worry." Don't worry about clothes or food—or anything else you need for everyday life. I don't know about you, but sometimes "don't worry" seems impossible to do. But here's a fabulous fact about Jesus: whenever he tells us to do something, he also tells us how to do it. And when it comes to "don't worry," Jesus says, "Look around!"

God takes care of his creation.

Just look at the animals. Lions have manes, clams have shells, and bears have coats. And just look at the flowers too! Their petals come in all shapes and sizes. They bloom in every color you can think of—and a few you've never even seen. From the fanciest roses to the dandelion weed, not even King Solomon, the richest of all the kings, had a robe as beautiful as one of these (Matthew 6:29).

The animals don't drive tractors, plant fields, or order pizza for delivery. But God makes sure they have what they need to eat. Anteaters have ants. Birds have seeds and big, juicy worms. And the panda has its bamboo. God loves all these animals, but not nearly as much as he loves you.

You're more important to him than any anteater, bird, or panda. More precious than any lion, clam, or bear. And more beautiful than any flower. So you can be sure that he will take care of you.

Just ask God, and he will give you what you need (Matthew 7:7). Does that mean you'll have your favorite dinner every night and the coolest of clothes to wear? No, but it does mean that God is your good Father, and he will give you what you need.

So don't worry. Just look around!

IT'S YOUR TURN!

God can use you to give people what they need.
Instead of gifts on your birthday, ask for cans of
food for a food bank. Share the clothes you've
outgrown. Look around. What can you do?

58

GIVE IT A NAME

Jesus asked him, "What do you want me to do for you?"

LUKE 18:40–41

A blind man sat by the road, begging for money. He heard a crowd of people coming and asked, "What is happening?"

"Jesus is coming!" the people said.

The blind man had heard about Jesus. He could heal people! So he cried out, "Jesus, Son of David! Please help me!"

Jesus stopped. "Bring the blind man to me!" he said. Then Jesus asked, "What do you want me to do for you?"

He said, "Lord, I want to see again" (Luke 18:35–43).

Jesus healed the man because he believed. But why did Jesus ask the man what he wanted? Because Jesus wanted the man to tell him exactly what he needed. Jesus wanted him to give a name to what he was asking for.

Jesus wants you to do the same thing. Why?

- When you give a name to what you're asking for, it means you've thought about it. You're serious about wanting it. You're not asking for God to "make everything all right." You're telling him exactly where you need help.
- When you name what you need, it gives you the chance to see God at work. For example, if you tell God you need help forgiving someone, you'll know he's answering when he takes away the anger in your heart.
- Naming what you need is also a way to give your worries to God. If you tell God you need help making friends, you don't have to worry about it. You can know that he's working on it and will take care of it in just the right way.

Be careful, though. Naming the things you want God to help you with doesn't mean giving him a list of demands. Instead, ask God for what you need, and then thank him for all he has already done—and for all the things he is going to do.

IT'S YOUR TURN!

Before your next prayer, take a minute to name the things you want to ask God for. You might even want to write them down! Then wait to see how God answers your prayers. Does he give you just what you asked for? Or something even better?

59

TWO BUILDERS

"Everyone who hears my words and obeys them is like a wise man who built his house on rock."

MATTHEW 7:24 NCV

Jesus once told a story about two builders. One was wise and one was foolish. The wise builder built his house on solid rock. The wind blew, the rains came, and the water rose up all around him. But that house didn't fall. Because it was built on rock.

The other builder was not so wise. This foolish guy decided to build his house on the sand. Maybe it was easier. Maybe he didn't have to travel as far for supplies. Maybe he liked the view. But when the winds blew and the rains came and the water rose up all around him, that house came crashing down.

What did Jesus mean by this story? Who are the builders? And what are the rocks and the sand?

The builders are you and me and everyone. We're all building our lives. The question is, are we building our lives on rock or on sand?

The sand is the world. When we listen to the world and let it tell us what is important, that's like building our house on sand. Because just like sand, the world is always moving and changing. If you count on being the best soccer player, the smartest kid in the class, or the most popular to make you feel important and special, then your house is sitting on sand. What if you sprain your ankle? What if you flunk the test? What if the cool kids decide someone else is more popular? The sand will shift, and your house will come crashing down!

The rock is God. If you let him tell you why you are important and special, then you've built your life on rock. Because God never changes. Make him the most important thing in your life, and no storm of life—no flunked test, no lost friend, nothing in this world—will be able to knock you down.

PRAY

Lord, help me not to build my life on unimportant things.
Teach me, instead, to build my life on you. Amen.

60

THREE LITTLE WORDS

I will give thanks to you, LORD, with all my heart; I will tell of all your wonderful deeds.

PSALM 9:1 NIV

Jesus was on his way to Jerusalem when he came to a small town. There he met ten men. Each of them had leprosy, a terrible skin disease. They didn't get too close—they knew people were afraid of catching their disease. So they shouted out to Jesus, "Master! Please help us!" (Luke 17:13).

Jesus saw the men and said, "Go and show yourselves to the priests" (v. 14).

As the men were walking away, they were healed. One of the men saw his healed skin and ran back to Jesus. He dropped down at Jesus' feet and thanked him over and over again. (This man was a Samaritan—an enemy of the Jews.)

Jesus looked down at the man and said, "Ten men were healed;

where are the other nine? Is this Samaritan the only one who came back to thank God?" (v. 17–18).

I'm guessing the other nine lepers were really glad they were healed too. But they were busy running to show themselves to the priest. They didn't have time to stop and be thankful to the one who had answered their prayers.

It's easy to see how those nine lepers are wrong. But how often are we just like them? Pay attention to your prayers. How many times do you say, "help me," "please give me," and "show me"? Then, when God does help you, give you, and show you, how many times do you remember to say those three little words: "Thank you, Lord!"?

If you want to be happier in your relationship with Jesus—if you want to just *be* happier—start with those three little words: "Thank you, Lord." And if people ask what you have to be so happy about, tell them about Jesus.

IT'S YOUR TURN!

Grab a notebook and start to fill it up with lists and pictures
of all the things you are thankful for. It can be people,
places, things, events—anything that makes you smile.
Decorate the cover with a great big "Thank you, God!"

61

YOU'VE GOT SOMETHING IN YOUR EYE

"Why do you notice the little piece of dust that is in your brother's eye, but you don't notice the big piece of wood that is in your own eye?"

MATTHEW 7:3

Imagine that you have a giant piece of wood sticking out of your eye. It's bigger than a baseball bat. Even bigger than a hockey stick. And everywhere you go, that giant piece of wood is bumping into stuff. It's smacking people in the back. It's knocking books off shelves and glasses off tables. But you've gotten used to it. It doesn't bother you anymore. It's like it isn't even there.

Your friend, though, has this tiny speck of dust in her eye. It's driving you crazy! How can she not feel that? How can she see anything with that speck in the way? Why doesn't she do something about it?

One day, you can't stand it a second longer. You've got to help her get rid of that speck. You walk up and . . . after knocking three books, a glass of water, and the cat off the table . . . you say, "Excuse me. Let me get that speck out of your eye for you." But when you lean in, your giant stick bumps her, knocks over her mom's favorite vase, and whacks the cat again. That's when your friend, who is just a little bit angry now, says, "Back off! Fix your own eye first!"

Sounds silly, doesn't it? But that's exactly what we do sometimes. It's so easy to see the things *other* people need to fix in their lives. Your brother needs to share more. Your friend needs to quit gossiping. And your cousin needs to stop losing his cool. While it's easy to see those "specks" in others, we ignore the giant piece of wood we're carrying around. Maybe it's selfishness or jealousy or pride.

The next time you think someone else needs fixing, take a look in the mirror. Ask Jesus what he would like to change about you.

REMEMBER

If you want to change the world, start with yourself.

62

GOD'S PARTNER

The Lord is close to everyone who prays to him.

PSALM 145:18

When I was about six years old and my brother was nine, my dad started building a new house for our family. But first he sat down at our kitchen table and drew out all the plans. My brother and I stood on tiptoe and looked over his shoulder. We gave him plenty of great suggestions. "What about a big window in the living room? Hey, you could put a swing set in the kitchen. How about putting a big slide right by the stairs?"

After a while, my dad put down his drawing pencil and looked at us. "You boys want to help me?" he asked.

Do birds fly? Do fish get wet? Of course we wanted to help! So every afternoon after school, my brother and I hurried over to the building site. We had jobs to do! There were kitchen tiles to unload, scrap wood to clear away, and stray nails to pick up. I wasn't just another kid in elementary school anymore. I was a partner with my dad!

Did you know that God wants us to be his partner too? God has a lot of work to do in this world, and he'd like us to work with him. Yes, that means you too. You join with God in the work he's doing every time you pray. You do it when you pray for what you need, when you pray for others, and when you pray for the world all around you.

Every time you stop to pray, it's like you're rushing over to the building site, picking up a hammer, and helping God build a little bit more of his kingdom. Oh, and every time you show up, you can count on your Partner to already be there.

IT'S YOUR TURN!

Just like with any building project, it's important to
show up and work every day. Pick a time to pray each
day—first thing in the morning, before bed, or anytime
in between. Then meet your Partner there in prayer!

63

SO YOU WOULD KNOW TOO

Jesus looked straight at them and said, "For people this is impossible. But for God all things are possible."

MARK 10:27

One day, some people brought a man to Jesus. The man was deaf, and he could barely speak. The people begged Jesus to heal him. Jesus put his fingers in the man's ears. Then he spat and touched the man's tongue. He looked up to heaven and said, "Ephphatha!" It meant, "Be opened." And the man's ears were opened. He could hear! He could speak (Mark 7:31–35)!

That was just one of the many miracles Jesus did while he lived on earth. He healed those who couldn't walk. He helped the blind to see and the deaf to hear. He stopped storms and walked on water. He even raised the dead to life again. And "there are many other things that Jesus did. If every one of them were written down, I think the whole world would not be big enough for all the books that would be written" (John 21:25). That was what his disciple John said—and remember, John was there!

Why did Jesus do all those things? Of course, he wanted to help those people. He wanted the blind man to see the sunrise. He wanted the deaf man to hear a friend call his name. But Jesus wanted much, much more than that.

He wanted these stories of how he healed and helped people to be talked about and written down. Jesus wanted the stories about him to be shared. So you and I—and all the people living more than two thousand years later—would believe that Jesus was more than just a good man. He was more than a teacher or a prophet of God. He is the Son of God.

Jesus did things only the Son of God could do. He did those things so we would know it was God who sent him. And so we would know God is able to do wonderful and impossible things.

PRAY

Lord Jesus, when I hear the stories of all
the miracles you did, I know you have the
power to forgive and save me. Amen.

64

THE BEST
INVITATION EVER

*"Whoever drinks the water I give will never be thirsty
again. The water I give will become a spring of water
flowing inside him. It will give him eternal life."*

JOHN 4:14

You get invited to lots of things—birthday parties, sleepovers, weekend camping trips. Some invitations are for a whole bunch of people. Other invitations are just for you. But there's one invitation that goes out to *everybody*. Even to this lady in Samaria, who had made so many mistakes that most people wouldn't even talk to her. Let me tell you about her—and that very special invitation.

One day, as Jesus was traveling through Samaria, he stopped to rest at a well in the middle of the day. A Samaritan woman came to draw some water. Jesus said to her, "Please give me a drink" (John 4:7).

"I am surprised that you ask me for a drink," the woman said (v. 9). Jews didn't usually talk to Samaritans.

"You don't know who asked you for a drink," Jesus told her. "If you knew, you would have asked me, and I would have given you living water" (v. 10).

The woman was confused. How was this man going to give her water? He didn't even have a bucket!

But the water Jesus invited her to take wasn't the kind that came out of a well. It was his endless supply of love and grace and forgiveness. Then Jesus told the woman all the things he knew about her life, and she was amazed. And when he told her that he was the Messiah everyone had been waiting for, she left her water jar right there by the well and ran to tell everyone in her town all about him.

So yes, you're going to get lots of invitations in your life. And some of them will be pretty wonderful. But the very best invitation comes from Jesus. Make sure you say yes to that one. Oh, and invite your friends too!

REMEMBER

Jesus invites everyone to join him.

65

NEVER-EVER-EVER

*"A thief comes to steal and kill and destroy. But
I came to give life—life in all its fullness."*

JOHN 10:10

The devil is not a good guy. At all. But there are some things that he is really good at. And one of them is what I like to call the Never-Ever-Evers. When something goes wrong, when you are having a bad day, or when you're just feeling kind of blue, the devil likes to whisper a few of his favorite Never-Ever-Evers in your ear. Have you ever heard any of these?

I'll never, ever get it right!
I will never, ever be good at anything!
The sun will never, ever shine again!
I will never, ever have friends!
I'll never, ever be happy again!

The devil's got a million of them. But I want to let you in on a little secret: not a single one of them is true. That's because the devil is a liar. In fact, he invented lying (John 8:44). Why does the devil try to spread so much doom and gloom? Because what he really wants is for you to never, ever, ever have love or hope or joy again. Not ever.

Like I said, the devil is not a good guy.

But God is good. He's always good. And what he really wants is to fill your life with love and hope and joy. That's why God has a few Always-and-Forevers that he wants to share with you.

God will always and forever tell you the truth.
God will always and forever help you.
God will always and forever be with you.
God will always and forever forgive you when you ask him to.
God will always and forever love you.

So if that old devil comes whispering his Never-Ever-Evers in your ear, tell him to be quiet. You've got God's Always-and-Forevers to listen to.

PRAY

God, I never, ever, ever want to be apart from
you. I will always and forever love you!

66

THE GREAT MESS

Christ had no sin. But God made him become sin. God did this for us so that in Christ we could become right with God.

2 CORINTHIANS 5:21

Have you ever made a mess? A really big mess? No matter how big your mess, I'll bet mine was even bigger! Or, at least, it was a whole lot stickier.

I was probably about your age when "The Great Mess" happened. My brother and I were playing tag in the grocery store. (Probably not our smartest idea.) We were running up and down the aisles. It was awesome . . . until I crashed into this huge display of honey jars. Jars flew everywhere. *Glass jars.* They hit the floor and honey flew everywhere. The store manager was not happy.

"Whose boy are you?" he barked.

I sat there, covered in honey. I looked up at the manager. I wondered how many years in jail I was going to get. Then I heard my mom. "He belongs to me," she said. "We'll clean up this mess."

Jesus feels the same way about his people when we mess up.

When you lie about studying for the test because you want to play instead. When you gossip about a friend and mess up your friendship. When you sneak around and watch shows you shouldn't. All those things make a mess called sin. It sticks to your heart and your soul. And it messes things up between you and God.

The good news is that God knew we were going to make great big messes of sin. That's why he sent Jesus—to clean up our messes. On the cross, all our sins stuck to him. He was punished for them, so we don't have to be. When you become a Christian—when you decide to love and obey and follow Jesus—you become one of his people. Then, when you make a mess, tell him you're sorry. Try not to make that same mess again. And know that Jesus is saying, "That one belongs to me. I'll clean up the mess."

PRAY

God, I'm sorry for the messes I make. Please forgive me.
And thank you for washing my sticky sins away. Amen.

67

WHAT DOES GOD DO?

"Anyone who has seen me has seen the Father!"

JOHN 14:9 NLT

There are days—tough days—when you might start to wonder about God. *Does God see that I'm afraid? Does he know I'm feeling lonely and alone? Does he care if I'm sad and hurting?*

The answer is *yes*! Yes, God sees when you're afraid. Yes, he knows when you're feeling lonely and alone. And, yes, he cares when you're sad and hurting. God sees, knows, and cares—*and* he's working to help you.

If you ever wonder what God is doing when you're hurting, just look at what Jesus did. Like the time he met a woman on the road.

The Bible doesn't tell us her name. She had been sick for twelve years. She had been to lots of different doctors, but they couldn't help her. Now she was out of money. She couldn't go to the temple to worship because the law said she was unclean. She couldn't touch anyone or hug anyone because then they would be unclean too. But this woman had heard about Jesus.

When Jesus walked through the streets that day, she thought, *If I can just touch his robe, I will be healed* (Mark 5:28 NLT). She pushed her way through the crowd of people until she was right behind him. As soon as she touched his robe, she was healed. And she knew it!

When Jesus felt the healing power go out of him, he stopped, turned around, and asked, "Who touched me?" (v. 31 NLT).

The woman was frightened. Was she going to be in trouble? She stepped forward anyway. She fell down at his feet and told Jesus what she had done. Jesus smiled and said, "Daughter, your faith has made you well. Go in peace" (v. 34 NLT).

What does God do when you're hurting? He does what Jesus did. He sees. He knows. He cares. And he makes you better again.

PRAY

God, you see me, you know me, and you care for me.
Thank you for always working in my life. Amen.

68

GRACE AND TRUTH

The Lord has mercy on those who fear him,
as a father has mercy on his children.

PSALM 103:13

There was once a father who had two sons. The younger son went to his father and said, "Give me my share of your property now." The father's heart was broken, but he split his wealth between the two sons. The younger son took the money and traveled to a faraway country. There he wasted his money on wild living. When the money was gone, his friends disappeared. When a drought hit the land, his food disappeared too. He got a job feeding pigs. The son was so hungry he wished he could eat the pigs' food.

The son began to remember all the feasts at his father's house. Even his father's servants had plenty of food. *That's it!* he thought. *I'll go back to my father. I'm not good enough to be his son anymore. But I'll beg him to let me be a servant.*

As the son was walking up the road to their home, the father saw him. He ran to his son, hugged him, and kissed him. And the father welcomed him home—not as a servant, but as his son (Luke 15:11–32).

That's just what God does for us. When we sin, it takes us far away from God. It can make us do crazy things. And we can end up in a place we don't want to be. But whenever we're ready to come back to God, he is waiting to welcome us home to him.

This is so important to understand: When you've messed up and wandered away from God, you don't have to be all "fixed" before you come back. You don't have to be perfect. God just wants you to come back to him. That's God's *grace.*

And this is super-important too: Grace doesn't mean you can keep on sinning or doing wrong things. God wants you back; that's true. But then he's going to start working on you and helping you be more like Jesus. And that's his *truth.*

REMEMBER

God gives us his grace and his truth.

69

TIM OR JIM?

When we have the opportunity to help
anyone, we should do it.

GALATIANS 6:10

Tim and Jim are as different as two kids could be.

Tim thinks everything is about him. He gets out of bed in the morning and thinks, *Who's going to get my breakfast?* He stomps his feet and pouts if no one wants to play his favorite game on the playground. And if his sister gets the last cookie, he's mad for hours.

Tim thinks everyone should try to make him happy. They should do whatever he wants. And the world should serve him. Since this almost never happens, Tim is usually unhappy.

Jim, on the other hand, gets up in the morning, yawns and stretches, and says, "God, show me who I can help today." He helps get breakfast ready and puts the dishes away. He makes sure everyone gets a turn to play their favorite game. He even lets his sister have the last cookie and grabs a banana instead. He smiles at the bus driver, waves to the neighbor, and asks the new kid to sit with him at lunch. Jim tries to bring a little happiness to everybody's day. Jim is usually happy.

Are you like Tim? Or are you like Jim? Or are you a little of both—a Tim-Jim?

Here's the thing: If you spend your days thinking everyone else should be trying to make you happy, you're not going to find much to be happy about. But if you spend your days helping others and giving happiness away, you'll find a little happiness—or a lot—in every day.

You see, happiness is a funny thing. You find a lot more of it when you give it away.

PRAY

Start every day with this prayer: God, show me
who I can help today. Who can I encourage? Who
needs a little happiness to come their way?

70

DO WHAT PETER DID

I said, "I am about to be overwhelmed."
But, Lord, your love kept me safe.

PSALM 94:18

Remember when the disciples were trying to cross the Sea of Galilee? A storm rolled in and their boat was in trouble. They couldn't get back to shore. Then, through the storm, the disciples saw someone walking toward them. *On the water!* Was that Jesus?

Peter called out, "Lord, if that is really you, then tell me to come to you on the water" (Matthew 14:28). "Come," Jesus said. That was all Peter needed to hear. He stepped right out and planted his feet on the water! One step, two steps, a few more—Peter was walking on water!

The Bible doesn't tell us exactly what happened next. Maybe a splash of water hit Peter in the face or the wind blew extra hard. Something made Peter look away from Jesus. He saw the wind and waves instead. They were so big! His fear became bigger than his faith. And Peter began to sink.

You may be a kid, but you can still have some pretty big problems. It might be a bully who keeps messing with you, your parents' divorce, or losing someone you love. Or maybe it's a bunch of little problems that pile up until they seem huge—like losing your homework, too many sports practices, and a friend who hurts your feelings.

When your problems seem bigger than you, keep your eyes on Jesus. Look at him, not your problem. *But* if you slip up, if you peek at that problem, and if you feel yourself starting to get scared and sink—do what Peter did. Shout, "Lord, save me!" (Matthew 14:30).

That long-ago night, Jesus didn't wait or hesitate. He grabbed Peter by the hand. Then he pulled Peter into the boat with him. Safe and sound. And he'll do the same thing for you.

IT'S YOUR TURN!

If problems are worrying you, write them down.
It helps to give them a name. Then talk to God
about them. He'll help you know what to do.

71

SPECIAL AGENT *YOU!*

Being with you will fill me with joy.

PSALM 16:11

The religious leaders accused Jesus of a lot of things. They said he had dinner with bad people. They complained that he talked to thieves and enemies of the Jews. They whined that he went out of his way to welcome people with bad reputations. And they were right! Jesus did all those things.

But no one ever said Jesus was a grump or a grouch. They never said he was selfish or self-centered or a snob. That's because Jesus hung out with all kinds of different people. He went to weddings. And he went fishing with friends.

The fact is, Jesus was a joy to be around. That wasn't because he knew all the best jokes or told the funniest stories. It was because Jesus cared about everyone he met. And he was never fake or phony. He never pretended to be like everyone else just to fit in. In fact, Jesus always told the ugly truth about sin. He commanded that everyone obey God's directions. But even though he was the Son of God, he didn't act like he was better than anyone else. Hanging out with Jesus gave people hope and peace. The people knew that they could always count on him to love and help them.

From the very beginning, Jesus has been on a mission to bring people joy. Now he wants you to join him on that mission—to be a special agent for him. You don't need a badge (though you can make yourself one, if you want to). You don't need a car or a plane. You just need a heart like his. That means instead of being selfish, give sharing a try. Think about how you can help others before you think of helping yourself. Go out of your way to be kind, to listen, and to simply smile. In other words, love people just like Jesus did. Just like he still does.

PRAY

God, send me on a mission today. Show me who
I can share your love and joy with. Amen.

72

WHEN YOU BELIEVE

*"I am the resurrection and the life. He who believes
in me will have life even if he dies. And he who
lives and believes in me will never die."*

JOHN 11:25–26

Martha had sent a message to Jesus days ago. The message said that Lazarus—Martha's brother and Jesus' friend—was sick. Martha just knew that if Jesus came, he could heal her brother. But Jesus didn't come. And now Lazarus had been dead and sealed in his tomb for four days. Martha's heart was still broken.

When Martha heard that Jesus was coming down the road at last, she rushed out to meet him. As soon as she got close enough, she said, "Lord, if you had been here, my brother would not have died. But I know that even now God will give you anything you ask."

Jesus said, "Your brother will rise and live again" (John 11:21–23). Martha didn't know how Jesus would make her brother alive again. But she knew who Jesus was. She trusted his love, and she believed in his power. So when Jesus asked Martha if she believed in him, she said, "Yes, Lord. I believe that you are the Christ, the Son of God" (v. 27).

Jesus asked to be taken to his friend Lazarus's tomb. He told the people gathered there to roll the stone away from the tomb. And then he prayed. After that, Jesus called out in a loud voice, "Lazarus, come out!" (v. 43).

The people all stared at the entrance to the tomb. Martha and her sister, Mary, surely held their breath as they watched. They might even have heard a little shuffling sound, and then—Lazarus stepped out of that tomb! That's when Martha knew that everything she had believed about Jesus was true.

Your faith doesn't have to be perfect. You don't have to understand exactly how Jesus is able to do the things he does. You just need to believe that Jesus is the Son of God. Trust his love and believe in his power—and he will do amazing things in your life too.

PRAY

Lord, I do believe that Jesus is the Son of God. Please help me love and trust you even more. Amen.

73

YOU MATTER TO JESUS

"Let the little children come to me."

MATTHEW 19:14

Do you ever get the feeling that some people think kids don't matter quite as much as grown-ups? That the bigger, taller, older people of the world are more important? Maybe they ignore you or pretend you aren't there. Or maybe they act like you're in the way.

Some people might think like that. And some people might even try to push you away—just because you're young. But not Jesus. Just look at what he did when his disciples tried to keep some children away from him.

It happened one day when Jesus was teaching. Some moms and dads brought their little children to see Jesus. They were hoping Jesus would place his hands on them and pray for them. But when his followers saw all those moms and dads with their kids getting closer and closer to Jesus, they stopped them.

"Jesus doesn't have time for this," they said. "He's much too busy and important to spend time with kids!"

But Jesus called out, "Let the little children come to me. Don't stop them, because the kingdom of heaven belongs to people who are like these children" (Matthew 19:14).

Not only did Jesus say they shouldn't chase the kids away, but he said heaven belongs to the people who are like them! That means that Jesus is looking for people who aren't puffed up and full of pride. People who don't think they're better than others. And people who will simply love and trust him.

It's true that some people may not have time for you because you're a kid. They might think you're not as important, not as smart, or not worth their time. But not Jesus. Never Jesus. He stands up for you because you matter to him too.

IT'S YOUR TURN!

Be a friend to someone who is younger than you. Play with them, read them a story, listen to them, and—most of all—love them the way Jesus loves you.

74

A GOOD GOD

Never stop praying.

1 THESSALONIANS 5:17

Jesus once told a story about prayer and why we should never stop praying.

In the story, there was a judge. He was not a good judge. He didn't care about God. He didn't care about doing what was right. And he didn't care what people thought about him.

In that same town there was a widow. She had been cheated by another man. So she kept coming to the judge and demanding that he make things right. But the judge didn't want to help her. (Remember, he was not a good judge.) Still, the widow kept coming. When he walked into court, she was there. When he left to get some lunch, she was there. She stared at him from the back of the courtroom all afternoon. When he slipped out for a snack, she was there. The judge even tried to sneak out the back door when he left for the day, but she found him anyway. And every single time the widow saw him, she said, "Make this right!"

Now, the judge was getting tired of seeing the widow. He wanted her to go away. But she just would not give up! He finally understood that the only way to get rid of her was to give her what she wanted. So that's what the judge did. Not because he wanted to do what was right. The judge helped her because she would not leave him alone!

Jesus explained the story to his followers. If a bad judge would do what is right just because the woman wouldn't stop asking, imagine what a good God would do—so much more!

God won't ever hide from you, turn away from you, or try to sneak out the back door. When you pray to God, he will always listen. He will always help you. And he will always do what is right.

REMEMBER

Never stop praying. God *will* answer you.

75

JESUS SEES

Jesus said, "Those who hear the teaching of God and obey it—they are the ones who are truly blessed."

LUKE 11:28

One day, Jesus was sitting with his disciples near the temple's money box. People were dropping in their gifts of money to God.

Rich people marched up and dropped in huge handfuls of coins. *CLANG! CLATTER! CLANG!* Everyone heard and looked to see who gave such great gifts to God. Others, who were not so rich, dropped in their coins. *Clang. Clink. Clang.* A few people looked up and saw them too. Then a poor widow stepped up. She quietly held out her hand, and two tiny coins dropped into the box. They weren't even worth a penny. There was no clang, clatter, or clink. No one saw her or heard a thing. Except Jesus.

Jesus turned to his disciples and said, "This poor widow gave only two small coins. But she really gave more than all those rich people. The rich have plenty; they gave only what they did not need. This woman is very poor, but she gave all she had" (Mark 12:43–44).

God told his people to give. And even though that poor widow didn't have much to give, she trusted God and obeyed him. No one saw, and no one cared. Except Jesus.

That's because Jesus sees all the little things you do to obey him. He sees you tell the truth when it would have been easier to lie. He sees you stop to help when it would have been easier to keep walking by. He sees when you pray for a friend, are kind to an enemy, and lend your neighbor a helping hand.

Now, the Bible doesn't tell us what happened next to that poor widow, but I believe as she walked home that day she met an old friend who said, "Come and have dinner with me." Because Jesus sees—and he blesses those who obey him.

PRAY

Lord, help me obey you and do the things
you will be happy to see. Amen.

76

BEST BROTHER EVER

"I chose you."

JOHN 15:16

My big brother used to pick on me. *A lot.* If you have a brother or a sister, you might know what I'm talking about. His name was Dee. And for Dee, he wasn't having a good day until he had made my day awful.

But there was this one time when he made my day *amazing!*

It was a hot, bright day in the summer. My mom had told Dee to watch me. He could still go to the park to play baseball with his buddies, but only if he took me with him. Dee moaned and groaned and even stomped a foot or two. Then he gave in. There was no way he was going to miss the daily baseball game.

We got to the park, and it was time to pick teams. I stood in the back. And I just knew I'd be standing back there until the very end. Nobody was going to pick Dee's little brother.

That's when a miracle happened. I just know that when the angels in heaven sit around and talk about all the great moments they've seen, this moment makes the list. *My brother picked me.* No, he didn't pick me first. But I wasn't even close to the last pick either.

When I heard my name, I couldn't believe my ears. "Who, me?"

"Yeah, you!" my brother barked, acting like he didn't really care. I strutted past all the other kids who hadn't been picked yet. And I stood proudly next to my big brother. The guy who'd picked me.

Dee didn't choose me because I was great at baseball. He picked me because he was my big brother.

When you decide to follow Jesus, God adopts you as his own child (1 John 3:1). That means Jesus is your big brother. And when it comes time to choose teams, he always calls your name. "Yeah, you," he says, "I want you on my team."

IT'S YOUR TURN!

The next time you're the one choosing teams,
pick that kid who is always picked last. Pick
them first and see how big they smile!

77

HELLO, NEIGHBOR!

Live a life of love. Love other people just as Christ loved us.

EPHESIANS 5:2

Every single law in the Old Testament can be wrapped up in just two commandments. The first commandment is to love God. The second is to love your neighbor.

That first commandment is pretty clear, right? After all, there's only one God. And he's so awesome and amazing that he's easy to love. But what about that second commandment? Who is our neighbor? Is it just the person who lives next door to us? Or could that law mean something more? Well, a long time ago, someone asked Jesus that very same question. And that's when Jesus told this story:

A Jewish man was traveling down the road from Jerusalem to Jericho. He was attacked by robbers. They beat him up, stole all his things, and just left him lying there in the dirt. A little later, a

Jewish priest walked by. He saw the man, but he didn't stop to help. Next, a Levite—a man who worked in the temple—walked by. He didn't help the man either. Then a Samaritan traveling down the road saw him. The Samaritan felt sorry for the man, even though Samaritans and Jews usually hated each other. So he bandaged the man's wounds and loaded him onto his own donkey. The Samaritan took him to a nearby inn. There, he used his own money to pay the innkeeper to take care of the man. (Luke 10:30–35, paraphrased)

When Jesus finished his story, he asked, "Which one of these three men do you think was a neighbor to the man who was attacked?" (v. 36).

Jesus is asking you that same question: Who was the neighbor to that hurt man? It was the one who helped the man, right?

In our world today, people are so busy pointing out all the ways we are different. We look different. We speak different languages. And we come from different places. But what Jesus wants us to see is that we are all loved by God. And that makes us all neighbors. So we should all be busy loving and helping each other.

PRAY

God, as I walk along today, help me to see *all* my neighbors.
And teach me how I can love and help them. Amen.

78

EVERY SINGLE ONE

Dear friends, since God so loved us, we
also ought to love one another.

1 JOHN 4:11 NIV

That guy? Yes. What about her? Definitely! And them? Yep, them too. Every single person you see is someone God loves. That's because every single person was created by God in his image. And that means every single person is someone you should treat with love and kindness.

Like Jesus did.

One day, crowds of people were gathered around Jesus. Then a man stepped out and bowed before him. The man was covered in a terrible skin disease called leprosy. The law said he had to stay away from people. He couldn't go to the synagogue or market. He couldn't be with friends or family. No hugs, no pats on the back, no friendly hellos. He even had to call out, "Unclean! Unclean!" to warn people to stay away from him.

But that man knew Jesus could help him. So he bravely made his way to Jesus and said, "Lord, you have the power to heal me if you want" (Matthew 8:2).

The crowds probably said, *"A leper!"* as they stepped back and snatched up their sleeves to cover their faces.

But Jesus didn't gasp, step back, or cover his face. He stepped *up* and he *touched* the man no one else would touch. Yes, Jesus healed the man of his disease. But he also touched the man's heart with love and kindness.

There are people everywhere who need your love and kindness—from the homeless lady on the corner, pushing her cart full of rags and bottles, to the lunchroom worker dishing out plates of mystery meat, to that kid no one wants to talk to.

Imagine what would happen if we all treated each other with love and kindness. There would be no more fighting, or crime, or wars. No more lying or stealing. And the world would look a whole lot more like heaven. What a wonderful change that would be!

IT'S YOUR TURN!

Change your corner of the world. Pick someone today
to be extra kind to. Tomorrow, pick another person,
and then another. Let the change begin with you.

79

GOD *WILL* ANSWER

"Pray to me, and I will answer you."

JEREMIAH 33:3

I love blue skies and rainbows. I love happy days and happy smiles. And I love for the people I love to be happy. Don't you?

The trouble is we live in a world where there is sin. Even though God made the world perfect in the beginning, when sin came in, so did things like storms, and sickness, and sadness. These are things you can pray about.

God will answer your prayers. Every single one. Sometimes his answer will be yes, and God will give you exactly what you asked for. Other times the answer will be no, and you may not understand why. But you can trust that he is doing what is best for you. Other times God will say, "Not right now, but I'm working on it for you." But God *will* always answer. Even if you don't see his answer right way. That's what happened with a father who was worried about his son.

Jesus had gone down to the city of Cana in Galilee. An officer in the army heard that Jesus was there. He lived in Capernaum—a long day's walk away from Cana. But the officer's son was very sick, and he knew he needed Jesus' help. So the officer set out for Cana.

When he found Jesus, the officer begged him to come back with him and heal his son. But Jesus said, "Go. Your son will live" (John 4:50).

The man believed Jesus and began the journey home. When he arrived, his son was healed. The officer's servants told him that the boy had been healed at the exact moment Jesus had said he would be. The officer and everyone in that house then believed that Jesus was the Son of God.

Did you notice anything about prayer in that story? Jesus didn't do exactly as the officer had asked. He didn't go back to the officer's home. And the officer didn't see his answer right away. He first had to travel all the way back home—trusting every step of the way that Jesus had answered his prayer. Jesus did. And he will answer your prayers too.

REMEMBER

God answers prayers.

80

A SECOND CHANCE

If someone does wrong to you, then forgive him.
Forgive each other because the Lord forgave you.

COLOSSIANS 3:13

Zacchaeus was a wee little man. In other words, he was short. But when it came time to collect the taxes from the Jewish people, Zacchaeus was large and in charge.

The trouble with Zacchaeus was that he was a Jew working for the Romans. These were the same Romans who were ruling over the Jewish people. The taxes Zacchaeus collected were for the Romans. And like a lot of tax collectors at the time, Zacchaeus often collected a little extra "tax" money and kept it for himself. He became a very rich man by cheating and stealing from his own people.

Nobody liked Zacchaeus.

Then, one day, Jesus came to town. Zacchaeus wanted to see him. Since he was short, though, he couldn't see over the crowd. So he climbed up in a tree. When Jesus walked by, he looked up and said, "Zacchaeus, hurry and come down! I must stay at your house today" (Luke 19:5).

Zacchaeus was happy, but the other people were not. "Zacchaeus is a sinner!" they complained.

Zacchaeus heard the crowd's shouts. He looked at Jesus and said, "I will give half of my money to the poor. If I have cheated anyone, I will pay that person back four times more!" (v. 8). Zacchaeus wanted to change his life. Seeing Jesus gave him the courage to do it.

The crowd that day didn't want to give Zacchaeus a second chance. But that's the whole reason Jesus came to this earth—to give out second chances to everyone who wants and needs one. And third chances. And fourth chances. And even seventy-seventh chances.

Are you willing to do the same? Are you willing to give a second chance even to those who have lied to or cheated you?

Because Jesus is willing to give a second chance to you.

IT'S YOUR TURN!

Is there someone you need to forgive? Pray for them and ask God to bless them. It's harder to hate someone you're praying for.

81

REAL SUCCESS

The Lord is all I need. He takes care of me.

PSALM 16:5

What does success mean to you? Is it being the most popular kid in your class? Is it smacking the ball over the fence? Or singing a solo? Or getting a perfect score on your book report?

For a lady named Martha, it was hosting the perfect dinner party. You see, Jesus and his disciples had come to town—to *her* house. The *Son of God* was going to be eating the dinner she prepared. Plus, there were all his disciples to feed too.

Martha hurried back and forth across her kitchen. How should she fix the lamb? Would there be enough bread? Martha chopped. And she stirred. But mostly, Martha got stirred up.

Why? Because she was doing all the work, and her sister, Mary, was just sitting! Okay, she was sitting and listening to Jesus. But she was still sitting. Martha got angrier and angrier until she just couldn't take it anymore. "Lord," she cried, "don't you care that my sister has left me alone to do all the work? Tell her to help me!"

But Jesus knew Martha was thinking about all the wrong things. "Only one thing is important," Jesus said. "Mary has chosen the right thing, and it will never be taken away from her" (Luke 10:40–42).

We have to remember to think about the things that are most important—like learning about Jesus. And we need to give our time and attention to the things that last—like his love and our faith in him. You see, Martha's dinner would be gone before bedtime. Being popular only lasts as long as someone thinks you're cool. Smacking a ball over the fence and singing a solo are great—for a minute or two. And that perfect book report feeling ends when the teacher gives you a new book to read.

Real success doesn't come from what we do. Real success comes when we choose Jesus.

PRAY

God, it's so easy to get caught up doing all the
things the world says are good. Don't let me forget
that spending time with you is the best.

82

FOLLOW JESUS' EXAMPLE

"I, your Lord and Teacher, have washed your feet. So you also should wash each other's feet. I did this as an example for you."

JOHN 13:14–15

It was the night before the cross. But the disciples did not know that. They were gathered together with Jesus for the Passover feast. Their feet were dusty and dirty from walking through the city's streets. There was no servant to wash them. And none of the disciples wanted to wash the others' feet. They were Jesus' disciples. They were much too important for that now.

During the meal, Jesus stood up. He took off his outer robe, picked up a towel, and wrapped it around his waist. He poured water into a bowl and knelt down in front of the first disciple. Then Jesus began to wash the disciple's feet. He dried them with the towel and moved to the next disciple.

The disciples couldn't believe what they were seeing! What was Jesus doing? He was too good to be washing feet. Only the lowest of lowly servants did that job. But here was Jesus—the Son of God—washing the disciples' feet. When he had cleaned them all, Jesus put on his robe and sat down again. Then he asked them a question: "Do you understand what I have just done for you? . . . I, your Lord and Teacher, have washed your feet. So you also should wash each other's feet. I did this as an example for you. So you should do as I have done for you" (John 13:12–15).

Jesus served. It's what he came to do. He served in big ways, like dying on the cross. And he served in thousands of little ways, like washing his disciples' feet. If Jesus was willing to serve in even the lowest of ways, shouldn't we follow his example? Shouldn't we serve too?

REMEMBER

Jesus served, so we should too!

83

JESUS ALREADY KNOWS

*God shows his great love for us in this way: Christ
died for us while we were still sinners.*

ROMANS 5:8 NCV

The disciples were sitting around the table. It was the last time they would share a meal with Jesus. The disciples didn't know that. But Jesus did.

Later that night, Jesus would be arrested. The next day, He would be nailed to a wooden cross and buried in someone else's tomb. The disciples didn't know any of that. But Jesus did.

Jesus knew a few more things too. He knew one of his friends would turn him over to his enemies. Three would fall asleep in the garden that night—even though he begged them to stay awake and pray with him. And all of them would run away and leave him.

Jesus knew all those things. But he didn't get angry or scold them. Instead, Jesus got up from their supper, took a pitcher of water, and poured it into a bowl. Then, one by one, he washed the disciples' feet. He didn't skip over the guy who was going to betray him, the three who would fall asleep, or any of the ones who would run away. The disciples were confused. Why was Jesus washing their feet? "You will understand later," Jesus said (John 13:7).

I believe they did.

Later that night, Jesus *was* arrested. And even though the disciples had promised to never leave him, they all ran away. They were afraid of being arrested too. When they stopped running and dropped to the ground, what do you think they saw? Their feet. The same feet Jesus had already washed.

Jesus knew they were going to run away. He washed their feet to let them know he had already forgiven them.

If you're ever worried that you've done something too terrible, too awful, too hurtful for Jesus to forgive—the answer is you haven't. Because Jesus already knows. And just like he did for his disciples, he's already offered you his grace. All you have to do is say, "Thank you," and follow him.

REMEMBER

Jesus offers you grace—even before you need it!

84

JESUS PRAYS FOR YOU

[Jesus] is able always to save those who come to God through him because he always lives, asking God to help them.

HEBREWS 7:25 NCV

J esus prayed for his disciples. Before he even asked them to follow him, Jesus prayed for them all night long (Luke 6:12). When he knew Peter was going to be tested by the devil, Jesus prayed for him (Luke 22:32). And before he was arrested—when he knew he would be leaving them—Jesus prayed that God would keep them safe (John 17:11, 15), help them stick together (v. 11), and give them his joy (v. 13).

Jesus also prayed for you on that long-ago night before he was arrested (vv. 20–23). But that wasn't the end of Jesus' prayers for you. It was just the beginning. Jesus is always praying for you. Even right now, he sits at the right of God in heaven and asks God to help you (Hebrews 7:25). And when the devil comes to God and points out something wrong that you did, Jesus defends you (1 John 2:1).

Remember that the next time you're in the middle of a mess and wondering where Jesus is. It doesn't matter if it's a mess you've made with your own bad choices, a messy fight with your best friend, or a mess of trouble crashing into your life, you can always know where Jesus is.

Jesus is praying for you. He's asking God to give you what you need. You don't have to fix the mess, make peace with your friend, or clean up all the trouble by yourself. You have the Son of God standing up for you!

Just imagine: When it's been a really rough day, and everything seems to go wrong, Jesus says, "Dad, could you send down a little blessing for _____ today?" "Father, _____ could use your help today." "Abba, could you send a friend for _____ today?"

And you can be sure that when Jesus prays, all of heaven listens.

PRAY

Thank you, Jesus, for praying for me. Amen.

85

TORN IN TWO

Nothing can separate us from the love God has for us.

ROMANS 8:38

When the temple was built, God ordered the workers to hang a curtain inside. That curtain wasn't just an ordinary piece of cloth hanging over a window, like the curtains in our homes. It was made of wool and woven with blue, purple, and scarlet threads. It was as thick as your hand, sixty feet long, and thirty feet wide. It was a wall of fabric! And its job was to separate the Holy Place of the temple from the Most Holy Place.[5]

Why did these two places need to be separated? Because the Most Holy Place represented the throne room of God. It was where the ark of the covenant sat and where the presence of God was. Only the high priest could step inside—and then only for a moment, once a year.

That curtain did more than separate one room from another, though. It was a symbol of how God was separated from his people.

You see, God is holy. That means that there is not even the tiniest speck of evil or darkness or sin in him. And it means that he cannot be anywhere near sin. Unfortunately, people are full of sin. Which means people cannot be near him. That's why the curtain was needed: to keep the people separated from him.

But then Jesus came. He paid for our sins on the cross. When he died, the curtain was torn in two. Not by human hands, which would have ripped it from the bottom to the top. It was torn from the *top* to the *bottom*. God himself grabbed the curtain and ripped it in two. Now there is nothing—not even sin—that can keep us separated from him.

Jesus paid for our sins on the cross. Sin no longer keeps us away from God. That means you don't need a high priest to pray for you. You can step right into the throne room of God and talk right to him. There is nothing—not even sin—that can keep you away from him.

PRAY

God, I step into your throne room, and I bow down
at your feet. Thank you, God, for taking away
the sin that kept me away from you. Amen.

86

DON'T KEEP IT A SECRET

I am not ashamed of this Good News about Christ. It is the power of God at work, saving everyone who believes.

ROMANS 1:16 NLT

When Jesus died on the cross, it was Friday afternoon. The religious leaders wanted his body taken down before the sun set that day and their Passover celebration began.

A man named Joseph of Arimathea went to see Pilate, the Roman governor. He asked if he could take the body of Jesus. You see, Joseph was a secret follower of Jesus. He must have been a powerful man to be allowed to talk to Pilate. Some think he may have even been one of the Jewish religious leaders. But while Jesus was alive, Joseph pretended not to love him because he was afraid of those leaders.

Joseph wasn't alone that day. Nicodemus went with him.

Nicodemus was one of the religious leaders. But he also followed Jesus in secret because he was afraid. Nicodemus brought with him seventy-five pounds of spices to wrap Jesus' body with. It was enough to bury a king.

Together, they wrapped Jesus' body in strips of cloth with the spices. (This is the way the Jews buried their dead.) Then they laid his body in Joseph's own tomb (Matthew 27:60). The tomb was sealed with a stone. Guards were ordered to stand nearby. And the sun set on that sad day.

Pilate and the religious leaders wanted to keep everyone out. No one was worried about keeping Jesus in. But they should have been. Because on Sunday the stone was rolled away, and Jesus rose to life again.

At the cross, Joseph and Nicodemus realized that it didn't matter what those religious leaders thought. The Bible doesn't tell us what happened to them after that day. But one thing is certain. Their love for him wasn't secret anymore.

Some things are supposed to be secret—like surprise parties and birthday presents. But other things should be shared. Don't keep your love for Jesus a secret. Let the whole world know you love him.

REMEMBER

Don't be ashamed to show how much you love Jesus!

87

THE MORNING
EVERYTHING CHANGED

"[Jesus] is not here. He has risen from
death as he said he would."

MATTHEW 28:6

It was early on Sunday morning—the Sunday after Jesus was killed on a cross. The sky was still dark. Mary Magdalene and the other women who loved Jesus were slowly and sadly making their way to the tomb. The disciples were hidden away, still a little afraid of being arrested. Pilate, the Roman governor, was still probably sound asleep. And Jesus was dead and buried. Right?

Wrong!

Suddenly there was a powerful earthquake. And an angel came down from heaven. He rolled the stone away from the tomb and sat down on it. And the only things shaking more than the ground were the soldiers guarding the tomb—right before they fainted.

The angel saw the women and said, "Don't be afraid. I know that you are looking for Jesus, the one who was killed on the cross. But he is not here. He has risen from death as he said he would. Come and see the place where his body was" (Matthew 28:5–6).

That was the morning everything changed. For Mary Magdalene and the other women. For the disciples. And for you and me. Everything changed because Jesus was raised to life again.

Death was no longer the end. In fact, for those who love and obey Jesus, it is the most wonderful of beginnings—a beginning of life with God in heaven. You see, when Jesus died on the cross, he took the punishment for all your sins. You can be forgiven and made right with God again. And when Jesus rose up out of the tomb—when he rose to life again—he opened up the doors of heaven and said to all who would believe and obey him, "Welcome in!"

That was the end of death for those who love and obey Jesus. And it all started on a beautiful morning. A morning that changed everything.

PRAY

God, thank you for Jesus. I'll say it a million times more—thank you, thank you for Jesus! Amen.

88

BE ON THE LOOKOUT

Crying may last for a night. But joy comes in the morning.

PSALM 30:5

Mary Magdalene knew a lot about sadness and suffering. Before she knew Jesus, seven demons had lived inside her. But then Jesus came and drove them away. That's when Mary learned to be happy again. She spent her days serving the one who had saved her.

Then Jesus was arrested, nailed to a cross, and buried in a tomb. And Mary was filled with a different kind of sadness and suffering. All through that Friday night, all through that whole long weekend, she wept for the one who had saved her.

Sunday morning came, and Mary went to serve her Savior one last time. But instead she found an empty tomb. Mary thought someone had stolen his body away, and her sadness grew huge. As she stood outside the tomb that morning, tears poured down her face. When

Mary thought she saw the gardener, she begged him to tell her where Jesus' body was.

That's when the man—who wasn't the gardener at all—simply said, "Mary."

Just one word. Her name. And Mary knew in an instant that this was Jesus! For three days, Mary's whole world had been dark and sad and full of tears. Then morning came and her life was suddenly filled with the light and joy of Jesus.

Yes, there are sad times and hard times. There are times when all you want to do is cry. But joy always comes again. Keep your eyes open. Watch for it. Be on the lookout. Joy will come again. God gave us a promise that sadness would not last forever. And because Jesus rose from the grave, we know that God has kept his promise.

REMEMBER

Keep your eyes open. Be on the lookout,
because joy is coming!

89

GOD IS ABLE

The Spirit of God, who raised Jesus
from the dead, lives in you.

ROMANS 8:11 NLT

When the women found the tomb empty that Sunday morning, they ran. They didn't walk or wander around for a while. They ran straight to the disciples. Those women didn't understand what had happened yet, but they knew that Jesus' tomb was empty.

Peter and John heard the women's news and headed for the tomb. No walking for them either. They ran the whole way. John was faster and beat Peter to the tomb. He looked inside and saw the empty gravecloths. But he didn't go in. Peter caught up and—being bold as always—he stepped right inside. There was the cloth that had been wound around Jesus' head. It was neatly folded and laid aside. Then John stepped inside too. "He saw and believed" (John 20:8).

What did John see? He hadn't seen the risen Jesus yet. He saw the gravecloths—strips of linen used to wrap the body—lying there. They hadn't been tossed around or moved or unwound. No grave robbers had done this. Jesus had simply passed right through them and left them behind. Jesus had risen from the dead!

Why is that empty tomb so important? Because Jesus had told his disciples that he would be raised up to life again. And that empty tomb proves that what he had said was true. It proves that Jesus really was the Son of God. No man could win over him. Not even the devil could keep him down. And if the power of God is so great that it can defeat death, then you can count on that same power to take care of you.

God is able to do everything he has said he will do. He is able to keep every promise. So when he says he'll never leave you, he will always help you, and he will save you—God is able to do what he says.

PRAY

God, no matter what happens today, I know
that you are able to take care of me. Amen.

90

FISH TACOS

When they finished eating, Jesus said to Simon Peter,
"Simon son of John do you love me more than these?"
He answered, "Yes, Lord, you know that I love you."

JOHN 21:15

On the night before Jesus went to the cross, he warned Peter, "Before the rooster crows this day, you will say three times that you don't know me" (Luke 22:34 NCV). But Peter didn't believe him.

Later, the soldiers arrested Jesus. Peter followed them to the high priest's house. He stayed outside and tried not to be seen. But he *was* seen. Three people accused Peter of being with Jesus. And three times Peter said he didn't even know Jesus. That's when the rooster crowed, just as Jesus had said. Peter ran away ashamed and wept.

But that wasn't the end of Peter's story. After Jesus died and was raised to life again, he went looking for Peter. Jesus found Peter on a boat, fishing with some of the other disciples. The disciples had been fishing all night, but they hadn't caught a single fish.

Jesus told them to throw their nets on the right side of the boat. The disciples didn't recognize Jesus at first, but they followed his directions. And fish practically jumped into their net. Now they knew it was Jesus! Peter jumped out of the boat, swam to shore, and ran to the Lord.

Jesus was waiting for Peter near a fire. He had made a breakfast of bread and fish—old-fashioned fish tacos. Three times Jesus asked Peter, "Do you love me?" And three times Peter said, "Yes, Lord." Why *three* times? Because Peter had said he didn't know Jesus three times. Jesus wanted Peter to know he was completely forgiven for all three.

When you choose to do wrong, that's called sin. Sin is like running away from Jesus. But like Peter's three big lies, no sin is the end of your story either. Because Jesus will search for you, just like he searched for Peter. And he will always be right there waiting to completely forgive you—as soon as you run back to him.

IT'S YOUR TURN!

Jesus never stops loving you, not even when you sin. But you do need to reach out to him. Say, "Jesus, I know that _____ was wrong, and I'm sorry. Please forgive me." And he will!

91

A HELPER FOR YOU

*"I will ask the Father, and he will give you
another Helper to be with you forever."*

JOHN 14:16 NCV

If someone asked you who God is, you know the answer, right? He's
the Creator of everything. He's Lord over everything and the one
who can do anything.

If someone asked you who Jesus is, that's pretty easy to answer too.
Jesus is God's Son. He was born as a baby in Bethlehem. He died to
save us from our sins, and he was raised to life again.

But if someone asked you who the Holy Spirit is, what would you
say? A lot of us—even grown-ups—don't know how to answer that
question.

"So, who is the Holy Spirit?" you ask. He is God's own Spirit.
You see, God isn't like you and me. You're just you, and I'm just me.
But God is three persons in one, all at the same time. He's God the

Father, Jesus the Son, and God the Holy Spirit! I know . . . it's a little hard to understand. Here's the great news, though: we don't have to completely understand the Holy Spirit. We just need to know that the Holy Spirit comes to live inside us and help us when we decide to follow Jesus.

How does the Holy Spirit help us? Here are just a few ways:

- He stays with you always (John 14:16).
- He comforts you when you are sad or afraid (Psalm 94:19).
- He teaches you what God's words in the Bible really mean (John 14:26).
- He reminds you of God's words just when you need them (John 14:26).
- He helps you pray (Romans 8:26).

So if someone asks you who the Holy Spirit is, now you know what to say!

PRAY

God, thank you for sending the Holy Spirit to
help me live the way you want me to. Amen.

92

CAN'T BE QUIET

You are to be [God's] witness, telling everyone
what you have seen and heard.

ACTS 22:15 NLT

There are times when you just can't be quiet. And there are times when speaking up can get you in trouble, like in the library. But there are times when the trouble is worth it, like when you're talking about Jesus. That's what the disciples decided.

You see, after Jesus returned to heaven, they started telling everyone about him. The religious leaders didn't like that. They wanted the disciples to be quiet, so they had them thrown into jail. But during the night, an angel of the Lord came and opened the prison doors. Then the angel told the disciples to go to the temple and preach about Jesus some more.

The disciples knew that would make those religious leaders even angrier! But let me just say that when an angel shows up and tells you to do something, you do it.

The next morning, a man came running up to the religious leaders and said, "The men you put in jail are standing in the Temple. They are teaching the people!" (Acts 5:25). And sure enough, those leaders were furious. They had the disciples brought to them. "We gave you strict orders not to go on teaching in that name," the high priest said (v. 28).

But Peter didn't back down. He said, "We must obey God, not men!" (Acts 5:29). The leaders had the disciples beaten and warned them once again not to speak about Jesus. But the disciples just couldn't be quiet. They had to tell everyone the good news of Jesus.

It's easier not to say anything about Jesus. But the people of this world need him. They need to know about his love and truth. They need to know how to be forgiven and how to be a child of God. And they need *you* to tell them.

Some people won't like hearing about Jesus. Some people won't like *you* because you talk about him. But some people will hear and believe and be saved. All because you just couldn't be quiet.

IT'S YOUR TURN!

Telling others about Jesus takes courage. It's okay to start with people you know and then go from there. Practice by talking to your mom and dad about Jesus. Talk to a friend. Then see who God brings into your life—and tell them.

93

ON THE ROAD AGAIN

*"I will show you where to go. I will
guide you and watch over you."*

PSALM 32:8

Have you ever gone the wrong way? Maybe you meant to go to the library, but you took a wrong turn and ended up in the gym instead. Or maybe your "wrong way" wasn't about *going* to the wrong place. Maybe it was about *acting* the wrong way. Like having a bad attitude or doing things you shouldn't do.

When we go the wrong way, Jesus doesn't throw up his hands and say, "Oh well! I lost that one." No! Jesus tries to guide us in the right way. That's what he did for Paul.

Before Paul met Jesus, he thought he was headed the right way. He knew every religious law in the book. And he wanted to make sure *every* person followed *every* law. He didn't like those Christians following Jesus' new way instead of the old laws. So he spent his days rounding the Christians up and tossing them into prison!

One day, Paul headed for the city of Damascus. He'd heard there were plenty of Christians there who needed arresting. Suddenly a bright light shot out of the sky. Then a voice said, "Why are you doing things against me?" (Acts 9:4).

It was Jesus—and Paul was terrified! He was also struck blind! His men had to lead him into Damascus. But Jesus sent a man named Ananias to heal his eyes—and to show Paul the right way to go.

After that, Paul went back out on the road again. This time, though, he was telling everyone who would listen—and a few who didn't want to listen—all about Jesus!

We all take a wrong turn once in a while, and we can end up going the wrong way. But Jesus is always there, always pointing us toward the right way. And he's always happy to see us when we turn back to him.

PRAY

Lord, thank you for guiding me and helping
me know which way to go. Amen.

94

EVERYBODY NEEDS
AN "AWESOME"

*When you talk, do not say harmful things, but say what
people need—words that will help others become stronger.*

EPHESIANS 4:29 NCV

Way to go!" "You did it!" "Awesome!" Who doesn't want to hear those words? It doesn't matter if you just solved the biggest math problem in the history of all math problems, if you kicked the kickball all the way over the fence, or if you finished all your homework before dinner—it just feels wonderful to hear someone say you did really great.

Everybody needs an "Awesome!" every now and then. The Bible calls these kinds of words encouragement. They build people up and make them stronger.

Sometimes encouragement is telling a person how great a job they did. Other times, it's telling someone things like "I believe in you!" and "You can do it!" and "You've got this!" And then sometimes, it's telling *other people* how good someone is. That's what Barnabas did for Paul.

Paul was known far and wide for arresting Christians and tossing them into prison—or worse! Then Jesus met him on the road to Damascus and changed his whole life. Paul knew then he needed to follow Jesus instead. Paul was so excited about following Jesus that he wanted to meet other Christians and talk to them about Jesus. But those Christians were still afraid of Paul. *Had he really changed? Or was this a trick to arrest them too?* That's when Barnabas stepped in. Everyone knew and trusted Barnabas. So when Barnabas told them that Paul was a changed man and they could trust him, they believed Barnabas.

Guess what *Barnabas* means? "One who encourages" (Acts 4:36). A pretty good name, huh?

God wants each of his people to be like Barnabas and encourage others. Look for things people are doing right and praise them. Cheer on those who are trying something new, scary, or difficult. And say good things about people to others. Let's all be a Barnabas to someone today!

REMEMBER

When you en*courage* others, you give them the *courage* to be all God created them to be.

95

ON A MISSION

The God of peace will give you every good thing
you need so that you can do what he wants.

HEBREWS 13:21

Jesus had a mission for Paul. Jesus actually came down from heaven, stood right next to Paul, and told him what he wanted Paul to do. (How amazing would that be?) "Be brave," Jesus said. "You have told people in Jerusalem about me. You must do the same in Rome also" (Acts 23:11).

Jesus told Paul to "be brave" for a reason. His trip to Rome was not going to be an easy one. It started with Paul being arrested. Then he had to sneak out of town to avoid being killed! When Paul finally boarded a ship headed for Rome, it was a prison ship. And Paul was one of the prisoners!

Then that ship ran into a terrible storm that lasted for days. Everyone thought they were going to die. Except Paul. An angel came and reminded him that he was on a mission. God wanted him to go to Rome, and he would make sure that happened.

Well, Paul did get to Rome. There was a shipwreck, a snakebite, and a trip on another ship in between. But at last, Paul landed in Rome, where he told many, many people about Jesus.

Paul's trip to Rome may not have happened the way he thought it would. But he knew God had a plan and a mission for him. And he trusted God to make it happen.

God's got a plan and a mission for you too. He wants you to tell others about him. Like Paul, you might run into some stormy problems along the way. There might even be a shipwreck or two. Your "shipwrecks" might look like losing your spot on the team, losing a friend, or even losing someone you love. But just like Paul, you can count on God to help you finish the mission he has for you.

IT'S YOUR TURN!

Missions can be big and huge and faraway—like sailing to Rome. But they can be close to home too. Ask God what mission he has for you today.

96

STOP AND GIVE
IT TO GOD

*Do not worry about anything. But pray
and ask God for everything you need. And
when you pray, always give thanks.*

PHILIPPIANS 4:6

D o you ever worry? Everyone does sometimes. Worry is what we
feel when we're afraid something might happen *or* might not
happen—or things might not go the way we have planned.

Worry can be like a little seed that gets planted in our thoughts. It
can grow and grow and grow—until it takes over! Worry can keep us
from doing things we want and need to do. And it can keep us from
seeing all the good things that are happening around us. That's why
the apostle Paul wrote, "Do not worry about anything."

Now, maybe you're thinking, *That's easy for him to say. He was the famous "Paul." What kind of troubles could he have to worry about?* Well, plenty, as it turns out.

When Paul wrote, "Do not worry about anything," guess where he was? In prison! From the moment he decided to follow Jesus, people were out to get him. He was beaten and stoned several times. The religious leaders hated him. *And* it seemed like people were always trying to kill him. So, yeah, Paul had plenty of things to worry about . . . if he wanted to worry.

But in the very next line, Paul tells us how to get rid of worry: "Pray and ask God for everything you need." God wouldn't tell you to ask for something and then not give it to you. So in Philippians 4:19, he promises to give you everything you need! And God always keeps his promises (Hebrews 10:23). Paul knew it, and now you know it too.

What do you worry about? Maybe fitting in or passing the big test. Or maybe it's your parents' jobs or someone who is sick. Whenever a little seed of worry tries to plant itself in your thoughts, don't let it grow. Right then and there, stop and ask God to take care of that thing that's trying to worry you.

IT'S YOUR TURN!

Check out a couple of God's promises for you: Psalm 121:1–2 and Matthew 28:20. Which one is your favorite?

97

KEEP YOUR BUCKET FULL

Be patient and accept each other with love.

EPHESIANS 4:2

I want to let you in on a little secret: *life is kind of like a bucket of Ping-Pong balls.* Now, wait a second—before you go telling your parents that I'm telling you crazy stuff, let me explain.

Imagine you have a bucket filled with Ping-Pong balls. Pretend that bucket is like your day. And each Ping-Pong ball in your bucket is a moment of happiness that you get to have in your day. Whenever someone does something wrong (or that you *think* is wrong), and you let it get on your nerves, make you angry, or make you sad—*POP!*—a Ping-Pong ball disappears.

- Your brother hogs the bathroom in the morning. *Pop!* There goes a happiness ball.
- Your favorite shirt is dirty. *Zap!* Another one disappears.

- The teacher announces a pop quiz. *Kerplop!* One less ball in your bucket.
- Your best friend doesn't save you a seat on the bus. *Swoosh!* Bye-bye ball.
- The cookie jar is empty. *Plink!* Another ball is gone.
- Your mom serves brussels sprouts for dinner. *Double-Pop!* Wait . . . there aren't many balls left in this bucket.

One by one, the balls disappear, until all your happiness is gone. How can you be happy or help other people to be happy if your happiness bucket is empty? You can't. How can you show people how amazing Jesus is if you're stuck with a frown on your face? You can't do that either. That's why the apostle Paul said, "Be patient and accept each other with love."

That means don't lose your cool—or your happiness—over every little thing. Don't expect other people to always do what you want. And don't expect them to be perfect. After all, you're probably not perfect either. Don't empty out your bucket over stuff that really doesn't matter. Keep your bucket full so that you have plenty of Ping-Pong balls—I mean happiness—to share.

PRAY

God, when things don't go my way, help me
remember that I can still be happy—because
I get to hang out with you. Amen.

98

BE HAPPY RIGHT NOW

I have learned the secret of being happy at
any time in everything that happens.

PHILIPPIANS 4:12

When will you be happy? When you make it to the end of the school day? When summer vacation finally gets here? Or when you get that puppy you've been wishing and hoping for?

Maybe you've decided you'll be happy when you kick the winning goal, swish the ball through the net, or break the record for the hundred-yard dash. Maybe it's when you're the top in your class. Or maybe it's when the bully leaves you alone or your best friend moves back to town.

You can spend your whole life waiting on everything to be just right—so that you can finally be happy. And sure, those things can make you happy for a while. But before you know it, there will be something else that your "happy" is waiting on.

Paul had a different way of thinking about being happy. He just decided to be happy. Whatever he had at that moment, Paul decided it was going to be enough. The really interesting part is that Paul decided that while he was in prison. Yes, prison! Instead of a puppy, he had a prison guard. Instead of winning the hundred-yard dash, he was chained in place. And instead of a vacation, Paul was waiting for his freedom. How could Paul decide to be happy in such a place?

Simple. Paul didn't make a big, long list of everything he wanted and needed to have before he could be happy. He made a very short list instead. In fact, it was so short that there was only one thing on it: Jesus. Paul had Jesus, and he was enough.

So, when will you be happy? If you have Jesus in your life, why not decide to be happy right now?

REMEMBER

If you have Jesus, you have everything you need to be happy!

99

HOME SWEET HOME

I ask only one thing from the Lord. This is what I want: Let me live in the Lord's house all my life.

PSALM 27:4

People say "home sweet home" for a reason. It's because home is usually a pretty great place to be. *Home* is more than a house or an apartment. It's more than just a place to live or an address on a mailbox.

> *Home is where you feel safe and loved.* There's no need to worry or be afraid here. There's someone to watch over you and take care of you—and give out plenty of hugs.
>
> *Home is where you can be comfortable.* You can crash on the couch, sprawl in the floor, and slouch over your homework at the table.
>
> *Home is where you know your way around.* You know where the

cookies and milk are. And you know you're welcome to grab some—as long as it's not too close to dinnertime, of course.

Your "home" might be right there in the place where you live. Or maybe it's at your grandparents' place, a friend's house, or your favorite teacher's classroom. But *home* isn't always a place. It's also a person: Jesus. How is Jesus like a home? Because with Jesus,

> *you can feel safe and loved.* He's always watching over you. You can give all your worries and fears to him. And he'll wrap his love all around you like a great, big hug.
>
> *you can be comfortable.* You can crash on the couch, sprawl in the floor, or slouch at the table while you talk to him.
>
> *you know your way around.* You know right where to find him, no matter what time it is. And you know you're welcome to ask him for help anytime you need some.

Jesus always welcomes you in. And unlike houses or apartments that you might move into or out of, Jesus is the home you can carry with you wherever you go.

PRAY

Jesus, help me find my home in you. Amen.

100

WHO GOD REALLY IS

Give thanks to the Lord because he is
good. His love continues forever.

PSALM 136:1

Sometimes we forget who God really is. He's not just someone we sing about, and he's not just another character in our Bible stories. He is the real, living, all-powerful Lord of everything! And *that* is something to rejoice about. What does *rejoice* mean, you ask? It means *celebrate*!

No matter what is happening around us, we can celebrate who God is. And who is God? He is the one who created the whole world—the whole universe, in fact! God made everything, from ants and elephants to starfish and stars. He's the one who hung the sun and moon in the sky and told them to light up. Lions roar, dogs bark, and horses neigh all because God gave them their voices and told them what to say. He makes the seeds sprout and the waves splash. It was God who taught the cheetah to run faster than fast and the eagle to fly way up high. And it was God who made you and me.

God is the King of all creation. He has no beginning and no end. He has always been. God never changes—he's always good and loving and kind. He knows the answer to every question, even the ones you haven't thought of yet! Nothing is too hard for him.

God is in control, and that's really important to know. Because when troubles come along, many people worry or get upset or afraid. But Christians don't need to feel that way. We know God is in control. *And* we know he's always taking care of us.

God is more powerful than any problem. He is tougher than any trouble. He is stronger than any struggle. So you don't have to worry or be afraid. Rejoice and celebrate instead!

IT'S YOUR TURN!

What's the best way to celebrate God? Praise him!
Make a list of all the things he's done for you today.
Then say a prayer thanking him for those blessings.

NOTES

1. Frederick Dale Bruner, *Matthew: A Commentary*, vol. 1, *The Christbook: Matthew 1–12*, rev. and exp. ed. (Grand Rapids: Eerdmans, 2004), 29–30.
2. Kenny Howell, "21 Fascinating Appalachian Trail Facts," *The Trek*, April 10, 2014, https://thetrek.co/appalachian-trail/21-fascinating -appalachian-trail-facts/.
3. Bill Bryson, *A Walk in the Woods: Rediscovering America on the Appalachian Trail* (New York: Random House, 1998), 161.
4. Zach C. Cohen, "Bill Irwin Dies at 73; First Blind Hiker of Appalachian Trail," *Washington Post*, March 15, 2014, https://www. washingtonpost.com/national/bill-irwin-diesat-73-first-blind-hiker -of-appalachian-trail/2014/03/15/a12cfa1a-ab9b-11e3-af5f -4c56b834c4bf_story.html?utm_term=.23d11af6b3c2.
5. Henry Blackaby and Richard Blackaby, *Being Still with God: A 366 Daily Devotional* (Nashville: Thomas Nelson, 2007), 309.